Understanding Vulnerability

South Asian Perspectives

Edited by
JOHN TWIGG and MIHIR R. BHATT

INTERMEDIATE TECHNOLOGY PUBLICATIONS
on behalf of
DURYOG NIVARAN 1998

Duryog Nivaran, c/o ITDG, 5 Lionel Edirisinghe Mawatha,
Kirulapone, Colombo 5, Sri Lanka
email: dnnet@itdg.lanka.net
http://www.adpc.ait.ac.th/duryog/duryog.html
and
Intermediate Technology Publications Ltd,
103–105 Southampton Row, London WC1B 4HH, UK

A CIP record for this book is available from the British Library

ISBN 1 85339 455 6

This research and publication was funded by the
Conflict and Humanitarian Affairs Department of the
Department for International Development, UK (CHAD-DFID)

Typeset by J&L Composition Ltd, Filey, North Yorkshire
Printed in the UK by Biddles & Co, Guildford, Surrey

Contents

Preface and Acknowledgements

This book is just one in a series of activities carried out by the Duryog Nivaran network under its theme of 'Understanding vulnerability and capacity' – a programme of work which has also included an international workshop, the publication of a series of case-studies and the development of materials on community-based capacity building for use by operational agencies and vulnerable people. The programme aims to provide insights into the nature of vulnerability in South Asia and to stimulate activities to build up local capacities to withstand disaster shocks. It also aims to build up two-way linkages between policy makers and projects.

Apart from the introduction, the papers published here have been selected from those given at Duryog Nivaran's international workshop 'Understanding vulnerability: a South Asian perspective' held in Sri Lanka in August 1997. We would like to thank all those who took part in that workshop – presenters of papers and other participants – for their contributions to the discussions. We would also like to thank Duryog Nivaran's co-ordinator, Madhavi Ariyabandu, and the network's administrator, Savitri Panabokke, for their considerable efforts in organizing the workshop and supporting us in preparing the papers for publication. Thanks are also due to Vishaka Hidellage and Dharini de Mel.

All of Duryog Nivaran's work on vulnerability, including the editing and production of this book, has been funded by the Conflict and Humanitarian Affairs Department of the British Government's Department for International Development (DFID). We are grateful to DFID for this support and for the substantial funding it has given to Duryog Nivaran's work in general since 1994.

JOHN TWIGG
MIHIR R. BHATT
London and Ahmedabad, May 1998

1. Understanding Vulnerability – an Introduction

JOHN TWIGG

A MASSIVE NUMBER of people in South Asia is affected by disasters. Between 1971 and 1995 natural and man-made disasters (apart from war) killed 37 622 people each year, on average, in the seven countries of Bangladesh, Bhutan, India, the Maldives, Nepal, Pakistan and Sri Lanka. The average number of people affected by disasters each year in those countries during the same period was 76 427 702 (IFRC 1997: 122–3). These figures, taken from the database compiled by the Centre for Research on the Epidemiology of Disasters (CRED) in Belgium, are certainly underestimates, for they exclude the numerous small events that do not receive emergency relief from outside.[1] However, even as they stand, they compel us to take action to reduce the impact of disasters on vulnerable people.

This book is published as we near the end of the United Nations International Decade for Natural Disaster Reduction (IDNDR) which aims to stimulate effective national and international measures to protect lives, property and livelihoods against disasters. In many ways the Decade has not lived up to the high expectations that accompanied its launch, but it has certainly stimulated renewed research and debate on a number of issues, and it has encouraged more extensive communication and networking within the disaster 'community'. This heightened awareness and interest contributed, in part, to the establishment of the South Asian network Duryog Nivaran at a meeting in Kathmandu late in 1994.

Initially, the IDNDR's emphasis was on scientific and technical solutions, but by the middle of the Decade it was clear to many of those involved that the social dimensions warranted much greater attention. In the early 1980s research by the Swedish Red Cross had already demonstrated a continuous increase – decade by decade – in the number of

---

1 The database's definition of a 'disaster' for the purposes of entering the event is 10 deaths and/or 100 people affected, and/or an appeal for assistance.

deaths and injuries from disasters, and in their economic impact (Wijkman and Timberlake 1984: 21–27); all the evidence since then has shown that the frequency and impact of disasters has continued to rise (IFRC 1997: 116–119).

This trend cannot be explained by a parallel rise in the number of events set off by natural hazards – earthquakes, cyclones and the like (there may be a rise in the number of man-made disasters such as fires and technological accidents, but in terms of impact that is only a small part of the overall figure). What we are seeing is an increase in the effects of disasters on people. More and more people have become vulnerable to hazards because of changes in their social, economic, cultural and political environment and circumstances. This is most apparent in the economic pressures that force many of the poor to settle in cheap but dangerous locations such as flood plains and unstable hillsides, with only flimsy houses for dwellings; but there are many other contributory factors.

When it met for the IDNDR mid-term conference at Yokohama, Japan, in May 1994, the international community signed up to a new IDNDR strategy that brought social aspects such as vulnerability into much greater prominence, and at the same time recognized that more emphasis had to be placed on community-based mitigation pro- grammes – that is, on programmes that involved vulnerable people themselves in planning and implementing mitigation measures (IDNDR 1994).

Duryog Nivaran's work on vulnerability

Duryog Nivaran is a network of individuals and organizations working in South Asia who are committed to promoting an 'alternative perspective' on disasters and vulnerability as a basis for disaster mitigation in the region. This is not the place to go into these ideas in detail, but in order to understand how the network approaches the question of vulnerability, and indeed how this book came about, some features of the alternative perspective need to be explained.

Duryog Nivaran's outlook and analysis challenge the 'dominant per- spective' among policy makers, donors, and relief and development agencies working in South Asia. The dominant perspective treats dis- asters as one-off events or aberrations in the normal path of develop- ment. As a result, practical interventions tend to take place after disasters have happened. They also tend to be top-down and inflexible in their method, with weak links at grass-roots level and little involvement of disaster victims in decision making or implementation.

By contrast, the 'alternative perspective' sees disasters, including conflicts, as part of the development of societies – as unresolved problems arising from the very processes of development. From this standpoint it becomes clear that there is a link between disasters and the nature of society. Relationships and structures within society determine why certain groups of people are more vulnerable to disasters than others. It is therefore vital to change those social structures, institutional systems and attitudes that make people vulnerable, and to build up people's capacities to protect themselves against hazards – before the disaster occurs (Duryog Nivaran 1996: 5–11).

The network's programme of research and advocacy is based around five main themes, one of which is 'Understanding vulnerability and capacity'. Duryog Nivaran's members recognized at the outset that reduction of vulnerability and strengthening the capacities of people are key features of some of the most effective disaster mitigation and management strategies. A range of methods and indicators are used at present to understand these concepts and guide operations. It was felt that there was a need to examine their value and effectiveness, and to develop new methods and indicators where necessary. Moreover, as so much analysis of vulnerability has been based on experiences from other parts of the world, there was a recognized need to root this improved understanding in South Asian contexts.

The Disaster Mitigation Institute (DMI) in Ahmedabad, India, undertook to co-ordinate the network's programme of activities under this theme. To date, the programme has had two main elements. The first is the collection of case-studies for publication as a series of short booklets. This format makes the studies easy to read and distribute, and permits the inclusion of quite diverse material – the last feature is particularly advantageous in view of the diverse nature of vulnerability itself. Three booklets were published during 1997 and several more are in press or in preparation.

The second part of the programme aimed to encourage debate about the theme and to produce a book synthesizing that discussion. The method chosen was one that has been followed successfully by Duryog Nivaran in other areas of its work: a regional workshop would be held where researchers and practitioners could present papers and share ideas. The outcome would be published as a book for policy makers, academics, planners and managers.

3

The workshop 'Understanding Vulnerability: a South Asian perspective' was held in Colombo in August 1997. Those who took part came from Bangladesh, India, Nepal and Sri Lanka and included academic researchers from different disciplines, managers in disaster and development agencies, field workers and consultants. Over two days they heard and discussed a wide variety of evidence and ideas. Short summaries of all the papers presented have been put together by Duryog Nivaran in a set of proceedings which are available from the network's secretariat (Bhatt 1997b).

The scope of this book

This book is not quite as was originally planned. Back in 1994 Duryog Nivaran had a more comprehensive study at least half in mind – even, perhaps, new paradigms or conceptual frameworks for viewing vulnerability. In the event, a more common-sense view prevailed. There appeared to be little point in expending the great effort that would be needed to design new overarching conceptual frameworks or models, and in any case vulnerability is too vast and complex a subject to be contained easily within the covers of a single book; this is explained in more detail below. As editors, Mihir Bhatt and I were also keen that the book should be read by as many people as possible, especially by those involved in operational work; and we appreciated that long, academic treatises – no matter how important their contents – tend to gather dust, unread, on bookshelves.

For these two reasons it was decided that workshop and book should be based upon grass-roots realities, and that the book should be reasonably concise. The material presented in this book was chosen to be of value to everyone working in disasters and sustainable development, whatever their area of expertise or institutional home. It is not an attempt to view vulnerability in all its complexities but it does present a variety of South Asian perspectives. The picture it gives is, inevitably, selective, but it permits deeper understanding by bringing important characteristics of vulnerability into sharp focus.

Three of the four papers in this book are case-studies. They cover a variety of groups of people living in different parts of South Asia and all exposed to serious risk of disaster. Ela Bhatt writes about poor women in the towns and countryside of the Indian State of Gujarat who face a wide range of hazards, natural and man-made. The Nepali villagers studied by Ngamindra Dahal live under the permanent threat of

4

mountain floods and landslides. R. B. Senaka Arachchi also looks at a village society, in Sri Lanka's Dry Zone, which endures drought as a persistent hazard to its agricultural way of life.

The final essay, by Mihir Bhatt, is a typically thought-provoking discussion of ways of understanding vulnerability by learning from vulnerable people. It is a spur to operational agencies and field workers to improve their ways of working with such people, and as a platform for future action it makes a natural conclusion to this book. Mihir Bhatt's paper ends by reproducing one poor Gujarati woman's account of her own vulnerability: it is fitting that she should have the last word.

Concepts and realities

The word 'vulnerability' is regularly deployed in discussion of disasters. We use it so often that we no longer trouble to explain or define it. Moreover, it is one of those fashionable words in development – others are 'participation' and 'community' – that are used as a kind of shorthand for a variety of ideas and features. As a result of being used in this way, words soon become loose, imprecise terms. In everyday life, we cannot avoid such shorthand words, but they can leave us open to misinterpretation.

As a glance at the dictionary shows, 'vulnerability' is a word open to use in a number of contexts. According to the dictionary I have on my desk, something that is 'vulnerable' is something 'that may be wounded (literally or figuratively); susceptible of injury, exposed to damage by weapon, criticism, etc.' (*Concise Oxford Dictionary* 1976). My thesaurus groups 'vulnerable' and 'vulnerability' among words that convey the idea of being susceptible to danger or even defenceless (Roget 1966). In the context of disasters, the word and concept were first deployed by mechanical and systems engineers, and until quite recently the most common usage was to do with the resilience of different forms of construction such as housing, bridges and factories. Those from scientific and engineering backgrounds automatically place the word in this context when they read or hear it, which often leads to confusion when it is being used to refer to the vulnerability of people and society.

In the socio-economic context, 'vulnerability' is usually defined in a manner such as the following:

5

a condition or set of conditions which adversely affect people's ability to prepare for, withstand and/or respond to a hazard (Warmington 1995: 1)

or

concerns the propensity of a society to experience substantial damage disruption and casualties as a result of hazard (OECD-DAC 1994: 8)

To show how vulnerability fits into the overall disaster picture, a number of writers have used pseudo-equations such as: disaster (or risk) = hazard × vulnerability. An alternative sometimes seen is: disaster/risk = hazard + vulnerability. The uncertainty over whether vulnerability multiplies or adds to the disaster is revealing – I have even seen it written, to avoid the issue, as: disaster/risk = hazard * vulnerability.

In recent years, a good deal of effort and thought have gone into researching vulnerability: what it is, and the factors that cause it. Models have been designed for conceptualizing and comprehending the subject and the best of these can be valuable tools for both researchers and practitioners. As examples, one might cite the 'pressure and release' and 'access' models advanced by Blaikie, Cannon, Davis and Wisner that allow one to trace the 'progression' of vulnerability by working back from the immediate to the root causes, and provide a framework for investigating vulnerable people's access to assets, income and other resources in society (Blaikie et al. 1994: 21–72). DMI also has its own framework or 'matrix' for viewing the different elements of vulnerability and capacity, where vulnerability is seen as the lack of security in four key areas: food, water, work and habitat (Bhatt 1996).

Conceptual models of this kind provide us with a way of framing questions and ordering our thoughts but they do not provide all the answers, nor should they be used as a substitute for fresh thinking. Moreover, while they are valuable when it comes to understanding basic principles, we must handle them with care as we get nearer to the circumstances of real-life vulnerability.

Vulnerability is too complicated to be captured by models and frameworks. There are so many dimensions to it: economic, social, demographic, political and psychological. There are so many factors making people vulnerable: not just a range of immediate causes but – if one analyses the subject fully – a host of root causes too. There are no common measures or indicators of vulnerability. At Duryog Nivaran's workshop, Madhavi Ariyabandu, the network's co-ordinator, pointed out just some of the problems that arise as soon as one tries to 'map' vulnerability in practice:

> Vulnerability is complex to map: how do you draw boundaries to vulnerable areas? Will these boundaries be geographic or administrative or economic or even from sacred geography? Similarly, what should be the unit of analysis? A family or a village, a community or labour force? Further, how to compare one type of vulnerability with another type? (Bhatt 1997b)

These difficulties arise because investigations of vulnerability are investigations into the workings of human society, and human societies are complex – so complex and diverse that they easily break out of any attempts to confine them within neatly drawn frameworks, categories and definitions. They are also dynamic, in a state of constant change, and, because they are complex and diverse, all the elements within societies are moving, so that these changes occur in different parts of society, in different ways and at different times. Mihir Bhatt, in his introductory address to the workshop's participants, also drew attention to this, remarking that:

> Especially in South Asia, multiple pasts and presents of vulnerability co-exist, interact and collide, as do Western and indigenous systems of knowledge, belief and practice of coping with disasters (Bhatt 1997a).

Even when we get down to grass-roots level, to studying and working with small-scale communities, we soon learn that 'the community' is not a single, homogeneous entity either but a dynamic mix of different groups, forces and attitudes – an important lesson for those advocating community-based approaches to development and disaster mitigation (Mitchell 1997).

Many of these complexities are evident in the case-studies published in this book. For example, the Gujarati women profiled by Ela Bhatt are well aware that their economic weaknesses of different kinds combine with the additional pressures that come from being women in a society dominated by men to make them vulnerable or keep them so. They perceive the dynamic pressures in operation and the root causes that lie behind them.

At Rampur, the mountain village in Nepal studied by Ngamindra Dahal, the twin hazards of floods and landslides pose a constant threat to lives and livelihoods. The villagers' land management practices are designed with that threat in mind, and they have developed a variety of

7

coping strategies to mitigate the impact of disasters; but their capacity to withstand and recover from shock is closely tied to the wider difficulties of managing a predominantly agricultural economy in a remote and inhospitable area. R.B. Senaka Arachchi has looked at another vulnerable agricultural community, that of Mahameegaswewa in Sri Lanka's Dry Zone. His study concentrates on the methods deployed by villagers to reduce the impact of recurrent droughts. Not only do these methods exhibit great diversity, but they reveal the extent to which the villagers understand their risks and plan carefully at times of drought, seeking to avoid practices that might leave them more vulnerable in future.

Learning how to learn

In recent years, professional people working in Third World develop-ment have often been reminded that their usually middle class, urban, academically educated and institutionalized backgrounds and outlook do not equip them well for understanding those they seek to help: they are outsiders, and to do their job effectively they should be ever-conscious of the fact. What is needed, it is argued, is a 'new professionalism' where development workers push their own biases into the background and bring the views of their intended beneficiaries into the centre of the picture (Chambers 1983). The now accelerating move in development programmes towards more 'bottom-up' and 'participatory' projects guided by the intended beneficiaries is a witness to the effectiveness of this current of opinion.

Similar complaints have been levelled against disaster professionals, too, and we are now seeing the first signs of a shift towards greater community participation in disaster mitigation and preparedness activ-ities. The logic for this shift is infallible: a project designed around the priorities of vulnerable people and drawing on their capacities has the best chance of success in the long term because the beneficiaries will be able to manage it on their own without continued outside assistance, and they will want to do so. To ensure genuine participation by the com-munity, development and disaster agencies are encouraged to use a 'learning process' as opposed to a 'blueprint' approach in projects. Put simply, the learning process approach starts from planning by benefici-aries and then evolves over time to incorporate different stakeholders' perspectives and to reflect the project's experiences. Blueprint projects, on the other hand, are planned from above and then implemented to a fixed timetable (Chambers 1983: 211–12). The learning process

8

approach is therefore organic and dynamic, reflecting the change and interaction that take place in communities.[2]

The value of such an approach in disaster mitigation is demonstrated clearly by the case studies in this book. The response of official institutions to disasters outlined in the papers by Dahal and Arachchi is a characteristically blueprint approach: the application of a static formula for relief that, while it clearly has some value, is not based on a good understanding of vulnerability or local coping mechanisms, cannot properly discern the victims' real priorities and is in any case only a short-term response to the symptoms of vulnerability, not its causes.

The papers by Ela Bhatt and Mihir Bhatt are both concerned, to different degrees, with the learning approach itself. Ela Bhatt shows how it can work in practice, and what it can teach us. Her paper is based on evidence supplied by women in different parts of urban and rural Gujarat who analysed the different facets of their own vulnerability quite extensively. By seeing vulnerability through their eyes, as they experience and understand it, readers of this book can begin a learning process for themselves.

Mihir Bhatt lays down a challenge to those who think they are already using the learning approach. He warns that outsiders, even when they believe they are guided by, or empathize with, disaster victims' own perceptions, may none the less still be imposing their own values on the evidence they receive. The very act of explaining other people's situations, or vulnerability, he argues, tends to smooth over the complexity of vulnerability and forces it into more manageable, consistent interpretations. The key to successful interventions by outsiders, therefore, lies in their admitting and accepting how little they understand of the victims and their vulnerability.

One way of ensuring that outsiders in implementing agencies of all kinds do become more sensitive to the needs and desires of vulnerable people is by introducing mechanisms that make them more accountable

---

2 Of course, this is an oversimplification of some sophisticated theories. It should not be forgotten, either, that learning process and participatory approaches are not without their own problems and can be difficult to implement in the field. Duryog Nivaran, as part of its work under another of its main themes, 'Understanding linkages with society', held an international workshop in November 1995 on the problems of 'participation' in theory and practice. The papers that were presented there have been published and make interesting – and challenging – reading (Bastian and Bastian 1996).

to the people they seek to help, and whom they often claim to represent. Many relief and development agencies alike are now beginning to think about this issue and are considering appropriate methods to enhance accountability. This is also one of the main themes of Duryog Nivaran's work. As a first step, the network plans to produce a manual on how the existing legal framework in South Asian countries can be used by people at risk to make official and other institutions more accountable; but clearly there is a need for a bigger range of mechanisms to draw upon. DMI has experimented with some devices, such as inviting victims of disasters to fill in 'report cards' on the performance of relief agencies. Much more work is needed to develop and test other schemes of this kind.

From understanding to action

This book is intended to stimulate effective actions to reduce vulnerability and increase security. Understanding vulnerability is just one step on the road towards better security, albeit an essential one. It informs our actions, but in itself does not generate them. Everyone who works on disasters has to address the problem of turning a sound understanding into effective, practical efforts on the ground.

As vulnerability is multifaceted, so an equivalent diversity of responses is needed to overcome it. Concepts can be deployed as a foundation for action but effective intervention requires much more: it requires appropriate methods or tools, and here too the range of such tools must be wide enough to meet the many different circumstances of vulnerability. Even the most flexible approaches to the design and implementation of disaster mitigation projects, such as the Capacities and Vulnerabilities Analysis (CVA) method (also sometimes referred to as the Harvard Method), or those based on Participatory Rural Appraisal (PRA) and similar techniques, need to be adapted to different places, structures and attitudes.[3] Vulnerable communities and those who work with them must be able to use these techniques, modifying them where appropriate.

---

3 This has become very clear from work carried out by the Oxford Centre for Disaster Studies (OCDS) to test and develop participatory methods in CVA. A similar method tested with communities threatened by cyclones in Andhra Pradesh (India) and the Philippines produced quite different results because of differences in social organization and outlook and, particularly, because of the different institutional cultures of the local and national non-governmental organizations (NGOs) involved as project partners.

One of the tasks that Duryog Nivaran has set itself is to promote such methods where they are already available and, where they are not, to expand the methodological toolkit by developing new approaches. The Colombo workshop took a first step towards this, and this activity should form a major part of the network's programme in the coming years.[4] It is of vital importance in reducing vulnerability in the region, and may be of great value to other parts of the world as well.

---

4 A brief overview of some participatory methods – for use in understanding vulnerability and vulnerability reduction – was given at the workshop by Arvind K. Patel from DMI (Patel 1997). Duryog Nivaran plans to produce more detailed fact sheets on each of the methods outlined.

2. Women Victims' View of Urban and Rural Vulnerability

ELA R. BHATT

NOTWITHSTANDING THE MORE recent, as well as increasing, awareness and concern among scholars and policy makers regarding the need for understanding the contents and the context of rural and urban vulnerability, through measures that can capture its extent and depth more effectively by using various methods and indicators, this chapter somewhat creatively collates the fresh views of invited poor women victims from rural and urban areas in Gujarat about what they mean by vulnerability.[1]

The views have been obtained through the use of the focus group Participatory Evaluation Writing (PEW) method among a cross-section of rural women from different regions in the Indian state of Gujarat and urban women from various *chawls*[2] and slum localities in Ahmedabad city.

The purpose of the PEW method is to find new tools for participatory evaluation and assessment by the local stakeholders – the poor. The tools are intended to introduce project management and policy concepts to the stakeholders, and to enable the stakeholders to evaluate and rate them. The method makes the poor central to the process and the tools 'democratize' evaluation writing. Each PEW is tailor-made for its specific context and purpose and goes through a cycle of joint reviews with the stakeholders: focus group meetings of 10–15 participants to concentrate on issues, joint preparations of PEW manuals in suitable language and

---

1 The paper is based on direct work by the Self Employed Women's Association (SEWA) with its 220 000 women members. I have also borrowed from SEWA's work on jointly understanding poverty with the United Nations Development Programme (UNDP) and the Government of India in March 1997, for which I thank the two, as well as Renana Jhabvala and Reema Nanavaty of SEWA and Neera Burra of UNDP.

2 Homes of the poor – mostly one-room, one-family accommodation, often in old and unsafe buildings with poor structures and few safety measures such as fire escapes. Women's security and privacy are repeatedly violated in such places.

form, two- to three-day sessions of PEW with 10–15 people and facilitators, one-day sessions to select the final PEW material, and the final text – edited by outsiders but agreed by PEW participants in a separate session. The introduction of topics is crucial. They are introduced in two ways: exploring by discussing related words and concepts; and letting the participants build a working definition and then move on to refine it.

Methodologically this is a new or different way of understanding vulnerability, and women victims' perceptions of it, and it does help in revealing some of the important components and dimensions of vulnerability and the conditions that sustain and perpetuate it.

The urban women are victims of floods, fire, health emergencies and riots in the large city of Ahmedabad and smaller towns such as Radhanpur or Anand. The rural women are victims of droughts and floods or both, or fire or health emergency. Gujarat has a diversity of geographical zones and climatic conditions: there are hilly areas, a long coastal zone and a wide network of rivers, as well as arid and desert areas. The natural hazards faced by communities living in these areas are similarly diverse: droughts (every third year in arid districts), floods, health emergencies such as malaria and flooding brought by monsoon rains. Man-made hazards include regular industrial disasters (in the country's most industrialized area), and occasional caste and religious riots. Due to particular patterns of development, in the past few years new patterns of disaster have become common, such as repeated floods in arid areas and multiple disasters (drought and floods).

Rural victims

Irrespective of regional variations in morphology, culture and climatic conditions prevalent in rural Gujarat, the women identified that their vulnerability was due to:

o lack of, or a weak or damaged, resource base (no or little agricultural land or water)
o poor resource quality (unproductive or less productive land, unirrigated plots or barren trees)
o lack of productive assets such as wells, bullocks and poultry
o lack of access to better seeds, fertilizers and channels of marketing
o near absence of activities in the non-farm sector
o high degree of indebtedness due to borrowing to meet various relief,

rehabilitation, consumption and social needs (especially dole, relief, marriages, births and deaths)
ס irregular and seasonal availability of wage labour before and after a disaster
ס low wages received.

The women added that their situation was also caused, as well as compounded, by:

ס illiteracy, lack of education and information on disasters (beyond their direct experience)
ס lack of awareness of different government schemes and programmes of relief or vulnerability reduction
ס rigidities of relief distribution under government programmes
ס incapability of raising and absorbing loans as victims from formal sector credit institutions
ס a not-so-sensitive bureaucracy
ס leakages to other groups, of benefits meant for the victims
ס prevalent malpractices in support institutions such as relief agencies and the civil supply department that runs the Government of India's Public (food) Distribution Scheme
ס the role of middlemen in the rehabilitation efforts, and individual or government income-generating activities
ס economic exploitation by non-victims
ס the patriarchy prevalent within the relief-to-rehabilitation cycle.

While the reasons listed were not identified in the order given above, these emerged out of what the women narrated or highlighted individually and in chorus. Some said that those with formal education and a job were not vulnerable. Others stated that even some educated women were vulnerable, but a majority felt that those entirely uncertain about their next meal were the worst hit. It was also opined that while all the unemployed were vulnerable, there were women who in spite of hard work were not better off either, for they received rather low and irregular wages before a disaster which made it difficult for them to absorb any loss. In spite of the enforcement of the Minimum Wages Act, they remained at the mercy of those on whose farms and firms they worked – and the jobs came so infrequently. Relief Camps do not follow minimum wages rules. A group of women from the deserts of Kutch stated that:

On the one hand, the prices of most essential commodities are rising and on the other our agricultural plots have remained unproductive,

14

lacking irrigation facilities and better seed supports[3] for a long time. The returns that we receive from agriculture are meagre, which forces us to go in search of wage labour that is difficult to come by, for agriculture itself is poorly developed in our region. We rise early in the morning, attend to the needs of men and children and start for farm-work before 8 a.m. By that time the ration shops are not open and in spite of adjusting our time and making efforts, we miss our quota of grain and kerosene. The shop owners deliberately pile up the stock and sell the same on the black market. Even the government drought relief scheme is almost of no help as it only ensures a job for a single member of the household. The situation is difficult to cope with and we are in desperate need of quenching the thirst of our land for water and hands[4] for work.

The rocky land and weak topsoil of the eastern hilly tribal region and northern drought-prone districts of the state have pushed people to the margins of vulnerability and compelled many to migrate in search of work, individually or in families. In a large number of cases, women are either left behind or participate in uncertain sojourns away with their menfolk with the sole aim of earning whatever wages are available from the unorganized sectors in an economy that is itself marred by disasters. They work in towns, cities or agriculturally rich areas with fluctuating wages and irregular jobs. Even among the tribals, the *Naikas* and the *Vasavas*[5] are the worst hit. In the words of some tribal women:

Vulnerability is caused and perpetuated by landlessness and the poor quality of land, which pushes us out to fend for jobs in different sectors and places. Relief is never enough to keep up work or life. We often move like nomads without a proper roof over our heads or a guarantee of our next wage, job or at times even a meal. We are cheated over our wages, especially by the contractors or *mukadams* [supervisors] at the construction sites and only paid meagre wages. How can we even think of sending our children to schools, or afford to seek and provide any health care for ourselves or the other sick, old or disabled members in the family?

---

3 i.e. timely, affordable supplies of seeds either from the market or from a range of government or co-operative agencies.

4 i.e. manual labour.

5 Tribals are indigenous peoples, as defined under the Indian constitution. *Naikas* and *Vasavas* are tribal communities originating from the hilly belt of eastern Gujarat.

The experiences of women from drought-prone districts like Banaskantha, Surendranagar and areas of Mahesana were not very different. Unproductive and barren land, the absence of irrigation facilities, low and uncertain rainfall and lack of productive assets drive them out of their homes for seasonal 'wage-hunting'. Even those with land have to seek wage labour, which is not available for more than 90 days a year. The general backwardness of the district is also caused by lack of growth in the non-farm sector as well as poor industrial growth. These add to the difficulty of working out a survival mechanism for most of the year. With a very high rate of landlessness and unemployment, the *Kolis* and *Garasias*[6] in this region are placed on the lowest rungs of the social and economic order. Significantly, those *Garasia* households having no male support find it very difficult to survive, for the women among them are not supposed to go out of their houses.

Even in the prosperous agricultural tract of Kheda District, exploitation of workers is rampant. This is especially true of the *khali* (tobacco growing and processing) workers, who work for more than 12 hours a day in depressing environmental conditions with very low wages and are compelled to provide a great deal of unpaid labour to the owners. Most are afraid to organize and fight for their rights as the owners' guilds are strong enough to throw them out of their jobs at any moment. In this context, the narration of a young woman is revealing:

stuffed in a workers' hut, me and my husband had to do a good deal of work for the *sheth* [money lender]. The tasks ranged from stacking and filling sacks of tobacco to sorting them out; and all tasks done during the night were never paid for. A paltry wage of 10 rupees a day was what I got paid for a gruelling as well as nauseating task lasting for more than 10 hours a day. Think of smelling of tobacco all day and night! Later they were compelled to raise the wage to 18 rupees, for we fought with the management through SEWA. During floods we lost our shelter. We received no wages. Since I was one of the leaders in this struggle, I was marked and one day when me and my husband were out at work, the goons of the *sheth* put out all our belongings, along with my old mother-in-law who was visiting us. Even the local MLA[7] threatened dire consequences if we refused to quit the premises. However, after the intervention of SEWA

---

6 These are also tribal communities in Gujarat.

7 Member of the State (of Gujarat) Legislative Assembly.

16

they had no choice but to allow us to resettle there. I feel that much of my confidence and strength has come from my formal literacy and my being part of the union led by SEWA.

Mortgaging of land and other assets to raise loans towards meeting expenses related to 'events' like floods, droughts and deaths is very common. The practice often puts many small and middle farmers into perpetual indebtedness. The group of *Parmar*[8] women emphasized that there was no choice but to spend around 5 to 10 000 rupees during a drought, for which they often mortgaged their land. There were several instances of land being mortgaged for more than ten years, for no household could escape spending money during a drought owing to the social pressures that emanated from their gnat[9] or caste. If they do not spend money on social events they are afraid of being cast out, which means losing access to the immediate as well as long-term community supports for relief; and naturally none could dare to do so. Some of them also emphasized that once entrapped in such private debt cycles, most could never come out of it in their lifetime.

There were narrations that recognized the positive potential of some government schemes but were critical of the manner in which they were being executed. For example, under the joint Government of India and United Nations Childen's Fund (UNICEF) Development of Women and Children in Rural Areas (DWCRA) scheme, a programme of small savings in some parts of the well-irrigated Kheda District began well enough but failed quickly as deposits were not collected regularly; nor was there any effective monitoring of the scheme during a flood year. Some women involved in raising saplings in the dry Banaskantha district under a scheme funded by the government's Forest Corporation felt cheated when the Forest Department lifted the saplings to sell on the open market during a drought. Some *adivasi* (tribal) women who had raised loans from banks to buy seeds after a flood were forced to bribe the sanctioning officer. One of them had to pay as much as 2000 rupees for being sanctioned a loan of 14 000 rupees. She was aware that it was illegal but had no choice but to part with the money, for she was afraid of losing the loan as well as access to such loans in future calamities.

Significantly, nearly all women from different caste and age groups

---

8 The *Parmar* community is in the government's 'other backward class' category.

9 A community within the caste hierarchy (sub-caste).

17

identified widows and deserted women as some of the most vulnerable groups in rural areas. According to them, such people were unable to secure family and kith-kin support and needed to look after their small children by seeking wage labour of any kind. At the same time, social and family needs did not allow them to pursue wage labour in all of its forms. The women also talked about malnourishment of their children and lack of, or very poor, health services in their regions, especially in drought seasons. Often the illness of an individual member not only deprives them of their wages, for they need to attend to the sick, but also at times a longer illness of an earning member can ruin a family's entire coping mechanism and stability, not only during a disaster or recovery but also during what are called 'normal' times.

While in their narrations the women from all the regions were articulate in giving meaning to the conditions of their vulnerability, it is important to note two key points.

The first relates to the fact that they were clearly able to see vulnerability as a product of a variety of deprivations and emerging conditions. Hence, their emphasis was on introducing efforts towards a multidimensional improvement taking place simultaneously in various aspects of their lives. The direct link between their ownership of assets and work security was very clear in their minds; so too was the fact that their access to various support institutions is related to their capacity to generate surplus that can be invested in education, healthcare, childcare and shelter. They recognized the 'cumulative causation' of such a process in leading to improvements in their life situations. To this extent they were able to distinguish between the chronic and transient aspects of vulnerability.

The second point was their ability to perceive their position as victims as well as women. Everyone among the groups stated how busy their lot had to be from sunrise till night in a variety of jobs like tending the children, cleaning the house, cooking, washing clothes and dishes, collecting twigs and fuelwood, cleaning the courtyard and cattleshed in addition to earning wages. During emergencies women not only had to carry the dual burden of productive and reproductive work, but also had to attend to mitigation, revival and rehabilitation. The pressure of work increased during sowing and harvest time, especially in small and marginal farm households that could not afford to hire labour, and also at times when there were guests or someone at home was ill or disabled. Contrary to the popular perception of women not doing productive jobs, we found that they worked on their own as well as others' lands in a variety of tasks that included threshing, cleaning, drying, storing grains, growing vegetables and winter crops, feeding the cows and poultry, replastering the huts with mud, stitching and mending quilts and mats, and a host of other jobs. Floods or drought leave them without this work and the income from it. And in spite of such a work-load their food intake within the household is often minimal, even during the pre- and post-natal periods. While aware of being victims of such malnourishment and of the internalizing of certain common and chronic ailments being part of their lives, they also identified that their vulnerability was related to illiteracy, no ownership or inheritance of productive assets, demands of dowry, social constraints in movement, male dominance, blame for sterility, constricted options and low wages. Sometimes the occurrence of an emergency was blamed on her!

The urban scenario

Living in different *chawls* and slums of Ahmedabad, working mainly in the informal sector and belonging to different lower Hindu caste groups as well as the Muslim community, the women from the city stated that they were vulnerable for a variety of reasons.

According to them, their poverty was caused and perpetuated by:

o lack of employment
o irregularity of jobs
o lack of employment protection
o low wages
o high indebtedness
o lack of sufficient and timely credit support for their petty trade and micro-enterprises.

The situation was further compounded by:

o constant fear of eviction in certain slum pockets
o fear of police and municipal authorities
o lack of relatives as well as community support at times of emergencies or crisis
o no (or meagre) family support for the old, widows and the deserted
o loss of productive assets and the killing of family members during riots
o the frequent ill health of earning members of the family
o expensive health services

19

○ lack of education
○ extremely congested and hazardous living spaces
○ near absence of essential services in the localities
○ prevalent alcoholism and drug addiction
○ a situation of despair caused by the loss of a more or less regular job of the husband or any other member in the family in a 'normal' or emergency situation.

Significantly, the respondents were able to identify that, even while being vulnerable, some of them were more vulnerable than the rest and some were near-victims or destitutes (there is a range of stages between being a victim and non-victim: for example, a woman may suffer mental trauma after a riot without actually having lost property or family members). They also highlighted that they were often driven to destitution by different crises in the household or city. A woman living in her 10 feet by eight feet *kholi*[10] in a slum narrated:

> I work as an earth worker at a construction site now and am not sure how long this job will last. Soon rain will flood the site. Shall I have five children to feed and no one for support? After being retrenched from his textile mill job some eight to nine years ago, my husband made several efforts to get a regular job but failed. Eventually out of sheer despair he jumped off the roof and died. I did not jump and ever since I have been all alone struggling to cope with my situation.

Another woman said:

> Around a decade ago our condition was better. But after losing his mill job, my husband nearly went insane. In desperation he tried to earn from whatever jobs he could, but was unable to get a steady job. Eventually he became violent and began to beat me frequently. For some time, I took up petty jobs like dishwashing and cleaning at others' houses but he disapproved of it. Fed up with his behaviour and scared of his beatings, I moved in with my brother along with the four children. It was the year we had plague in Ahmedabad city. Two of my sons are now at an *ashram*[11] and one is disabled. I wake up at four in the morning and after procuring vegetables from the wholesale market sell them in the lanes and by-lanes in and around the

---

10 A small, crowded, poorly ventilated room used by one or more families as a home.

11 In this context, a boarding school run by a charity.

locality. I buy rice and flour from my earnings on a day-to-day basis and cook food for the family after my return home at two in the afternoon. At times, I hardly have any money to buy essentials and the situation becomes worse when I am ill or there are riots in the city and I am unable to sell vegetables. All this makes me very nervous and uncertain about the future and I dread facing it every morning.

There were more women with similar life stories and it seems that the closure of the textile mills in Ahmedabad has pushed many families to the brink of vulnerability and near-destitution. Even two days of rain are as bad as a major flood for them. In a number of households husbands have become either alcoholic, drug addicts or quite disturbed and desperate owing to chronic unemployment.[12] And relief never provides employment. Often they are not able to supplement the earnings of their wives who are engaged in various jobs like carrying headloads in the *kapad* (cloth) bazaar, rolling *papads* and making *puris*,[13] paid domestic help, making *agarbattis* (incense sticks), envelopes and plastic bags for sale, vending, hawking, rag-collection and construction labour. All these jobs are more vulnerable to a flood or fire or riot in the city. Hence, many have not been able to get out of the debts incurred for marriages, loss of property, illnesses, death rites, or purchase of a hut, lathe or handcart. The fall in income has been too drastic for some and has shaken the entire family. Often such occurrences have compelled many to withdraw their children from school and marry off their daughters early.

Frequent communal riots in the city have torn apart and ruined many households. While some have lost their dear ones in the frenzy of looting, arson and killings, others have lost every bit of their belongings. Narrating her tale, a Muslim woman said,

Thirty-five years ago, I came to Ahmedabad from Gorakhpur after marriage. My husband owned a tiny workshop that moulded used plastic materials. We witnessed both the major riots of 1969 and 1985.

---

12 For example, a survey by SEWA in 1997 of families in the Textile Workers Housing Colony in Bapungar – where 85 per cent of the families are victims of the closure of the textile mills – showed that the men have resorted to drinking (36 per cent), drugs (2 per cent), wife beating (77 per cent) and become depressed (53 per cent). The burden of running the household is very heavy on the women: 73 per cent of them are the sole supporters of the family. Many are engaged in homebased piece-rate production for middlemen, mainly of incense sticks.

13 *Papad* is a kind of roasted spiced *roti* (bread) eaten with meals; *puris* are deep fried, puffed *rotis* mostly made of wheat flour.

During the 1969 riots – luckily – our house was safe, although we had run off to Uttar Pradesh for safety. But in the 1985 riots our entire house was burnt down and in spite of trying our level best we didn't receive a penny in compensation. We were not even able to raise a loan and could never rebuild our workshop. My husband has had no regular job for the last 10 years. One of our two sons works as a labourer on a milk van and the other is unemployed. I make *agarbattis* at home and am paid four rupees for making a thousand of them. During a day, I am able to make around 3000 *agarbattis* and earn around 350 rupees a month. Mine and my son's earnings together do not exceed 1100 rupees a month and I am worried about what will happen to us if our son does not support us in future. But that worry can wait. I think of another riot which can happen any time and I shudder. Which is worse? Now or the future?

There were similar tales from other Muslim women who had lost their productive assets like rickshaws, *laris* (hand carts), sewing machines and lathes in riots and were eventually compelled to opt for jobs like selling spices, vegetables and snacks, or garment sewing. It seems that many of the riot victims have not been able to return to their earlier economic position and have continued to experience sustained deterioration. The sudden fall in such cases has often incapacitated households by pushing them into a circuit characterized by lower and fluctuating earnings and a correspondingly lower quality of life.

Significantly, as many as 36 per cent of women among the respondents were sole breadwinners in their households and another 18 per cent contributed more than 50 per cent of their household's income (but when dole for work is given by non-governmental organizations (NGOs) it is mostly for men). The activities in which they are generally engaged include home-based work in the areas of production and processing, jobs in factories and wage labour in the service sector, as well as working in sales and petty trade. Some among them are old and alone, some deserted but living with relatives, some widowed but supporting the children and some living in nuclear family units. Two of the older widows living all by themselves in tiny *kutcha*[14] huts in different slums struggled for survival by trying to seek whatever jobs they could get. They could no longer do heavy manual jobs, and treatment for their chronic illnesses was beyond their reach. Desertion by men (on purpose or

---

14 Relatively flimsy building; not built to last

by default), which apparently is a common phenomenon in many of the localities, often forces such women to opt for alternative arrangements for survival. One of them who had migrated from Dhule in Maharashtra after marriage narrated that:

> Some six years ago my husband left me to live with another woman. I had no idea what to do and was scared to even look for work. I did not even know what work to do and whom to approach. I had no money to pay the rent and finally came to stay in another *jhupadpatti* [area within the slum] to live with my mother and younger brother who worked as a casual wage labourer and earned only too little. But my *masi* [mother's sister] helped me in getting a casual job of carrying headloads in the *kapad* bazaar. My brother is now often unemployed. On average I earn 25 rupees a day and the family lives on this amount in an eight foot by eight foot hut for which I pay 100 rupees a month. A little rain in a drought year can flood my room. The clay walls can melt at any time.

While a large number of the urban poor seems to live below the 'poverty line', the intensity and depth of vulnerability varies among them. Such variations are caused by permutations and combinations of different factors. The destitutes and the extremely vulnerable not only live with a perpetual sense of uncertainty and fear but also lack support from their families and the community. Some, however, are able to manage a shade better owing to regular or even fluctuating income, but never feel confident about crossing the poverty barricade. Their attempts to cope with their vulnerability while waiting for a disaster result in curtailing their expenditure on consumption of food and clothes, medical needs and children's education. This means more vulnerability. While the inelasticity of the labour market pushes many of them into the 'unemployed' slot, as well as keeping them there, a section manages to cling on to the job net by slipping and rising within the lower circuits of the economy. Such efforts appear to be *ad hoc*, but more often than not these manifest, and are sustained by, patron-client relations and kith-kin-peer networking where it exists.

The predominance of irregular and fluctuating income compels vulnerable households to procure grains and vegetables on credit as well as to remain indebted to friends, peers, petty-shopkeepers, small-time money lenders and employers. Their lack of access to institutional credit often makes them more vulnerable and keeps them entrapped in the vicious circle of raising loans and trying to earn and repay the same. The groups of unemployed or destitutes cannot even raise money from such 'informal' sources. Sudden medical emergencies or expenses incurred in marriage put some households in a situation of permanent indebtedness and many can never even recover their mortgaged ornaments. At times the pawn-broker runs away with the money and ornaments and this puts the families in an even more desperate situation.

According to a majority of the respondents, it is also common for children to supplement the family income by working as wage labourers. Girls often accompany their mothers or aunts as maid-servants, vegetable vendors and construction labourers; the boys work in small restaurants, sweet shops, cycle and auto repair units and roadside snack and tea *laris*. Many pointed out that with some money in hand, the boys begin to gamble, sniff drugs and consume alcohol. Some members of the group emphasized that marginal living conditions and lack of proper education among children were factors creating a socially and physically unhealthy environment which has led to the emergence of insecure and hazardous living conditions in the slums and shanty localities.

Everyone recognized that their living condition was related to vulnerability: they had only a limited amount of drinking water and nearly no space for a secure bath and defecation. Some sleep out, for their huts are tiny and yet expensive, with rents ranging from 100 to 200 rupees a month and deposits exceeding 1000 rupees for an eight foot by 10 foot *kholi*. The rains create havoc and the leaking roofs of the predominantly *kutcha* huts help breed a variety of illnesses. Rains also dampen earnings as it becomes difficult to carry on vegetable selling and petty trading, to store clothes and garments for stitching, or to dry pickles, *papad* and plastic, while expenses and debts rise in order to meet the needs of the ill.

Like the women from rural areas, the urban women linked their vulnerable conditions with the overall environment, which according to them was characterized by a lack of regular income, unprotected employment, marginal living conditions, poor quality of life and diminishing family and community supports. Widows and the old, the deserted and the chronically ill were identified as the weakest among the vulnerable. The fact that they still thought that life in rural areas was better than in cities indicates their vulnerability within the urban context. But at the same time, the possibility of a higher urban wage, hopes of a regular income and absence of any substantial resource base in rural areas keep them stuck to the city, its shanties and its ever-oppressive, constricted job market.

24

They are as hard pressed as their female counterparts in villages, doing all sorts of jobs at home and outside. They cook, clean, care and carry family burdens and headloads simultaneously, and at the same time remain marginalized by desertions and beatings and are often thrown out when old and invalid.

While a sudden job loss, drastic falls in regular income, a riot, a fire or the sudden demise of an earning family member can cripple their mode and manner of coping with disaster beyond redemption, appropriate supports that severally aim at raising their quality of life through a multiple improvement in their health, working conditions, education and legal as well as social protection, can make them graduate to a better position. This came out clearly when the group highlighted what they meant by vulnerability and how could it be reduced.

Conclusion

The preceding discussion brings out the differences in the nature of rural and urban vulnerability. As to how the women remain placed within these settings, their narrations and perceptions about vulnerability bring forth some important points.

The first relates to the dynamic that keeps them in a 'vulnerability locked' situation from which they are only seldom able to escape. The fact that individuals and households inherit vulnerable conditions is related to the lack of opportunities which can enhance their resource base and empower them to negotiate with and absorb market forces. Beyond a critical point their vulnerability increases progressively leading to destitution, and often only one crisis or catastrophe is enough for them to be pushed down the ladder. Subsequently this puts into motion a chain reaction of mortgaging property and distress sale of possessions and assets, and as a consequence the household tends to develop coping mechanisms that are weaker than the former ones. Many have no coping mechanisms. This not only marginalizes the entire household but the burden is often unequally borne, with women and female children carrying most of it.

The second point concerns when vulnerability compels women to expand their efforts to earn a wage (or higher wage), especially in the lower and informal sectors of the economy. This often makes them victims of a hostile and exploitative economic system and at the same time places them at the receiving end of domestic clashes and violence. It is noteworthy that the most vulnerable families are often women-headed households, many of these women being widows and deserted wives.

The third point is related to the cumulative result of such processes, which begins to erode community and family support systems. This is more common in urban areas which, in the first instance, house migrants from far and near. The social chord between rural and urban households begins to snap with diminishing mutual supports and eventually elements of disintegration set in, even within the immediate family.

Undoubtedly the above situation must be altered. And in order to do so the intensity and depth of vulnerability must be gauged through a comprehensive understanding of the components of the processes that produce and sustain it, with a widening of the range of methods and indicators that can capture the essential ingredients of its product. It is not enough to enlarge the list of indicators; they must also be sharpened through a series of intensive studies of victims and vulnerable conditions at the micro-level across regions. While integrated household surveys capable of reflecting the economic and extra-economic conditions of rural and urban vulnerable households are an essential data base for appropriate policy formation, their links with the qualitative aspects of life must be ascertained in order to have a fuller understanding of the association between vulnerability, life cycles and the quality of life. Most important in this is to find ways for the victims and the vulnerable to have some renewed sense of their own vulnerability and their current efforts towards reducing it. It is their improved, additional, and refreshed understanding, when matched with resources and institutions, that can reduce risk.

3. Drought and Household Coping Strategies among Peasant Communities in the Dry Zone of Sri Lanka[1]

R.B. SENAKA ARACHCHI

Introduction

DROUGHT AND dry spells are often caused by the failure of expected monsoon rains in the Dry Zone[2] of Sri Lanka. Such failures may lead to wilting of plants and continuous decrease in the levels of water in streams and reservoirs, resulting in shortages of water for agriculture, animal husbandry and even for domestic use. Rainfall fluctuations are, however, not a recent phenomenon in Sri Lanka. There have been many severe and widespread droughts in the past. The economic disruption, social dislocation and human suffering caused by drought among Dry Zone peasant communities have often been described in historical chronicles such as the *Mahavansa* and the *Chulavansa*.[3] In modern times, almost every year, the media report on the effects of drought on human life in many parts of the country.

The 'hydraulic civilization' founded in the Dry Zone by ancient Sinhalese kings displays evidence of remarkable human effort to mitigate the drought hazard (Gunawardena 1971; Siriweera 1971; Leach 1959; Witfogel 1957). The major feature was the construction of an intricate system of reservoirs (tanks) to store water for irrigated agriculture. Over 10 000 reservoirs were built at different periods from the 3rd century BC to the 12th century AD, scattered over the different parts of the Dry Zone. Their capacities vary from a few cubic metres

---

1 Responsibility for the contents of this chapter rests with the author and it does not necessarily reflect the views of the International Irrigation Management Institute where the author is employed.

2 The broad plains in the north and east are known as the Dry Zone of the country. The annual rainfall in this part of the country ranges between 1250 and 1900 millimetres and the bulk of the precipitation occurs during the north-east monsoon period from November to February.

3 The *Mahavansa* and *Chulavansa,* which appear to date from at least the 5th century AD and were compiled over a period of some centuries before that, trace the course of events over 2500 years.

to over 2800 cubic metres of water (Irrigation Department 1975). Many have been restored in the recent past and are again providing irrigation water for some 290 000 hectares of agricultural land (Department of Census and Statistics 1988: 65). The majority of these tanks depend on local rainfall and are therefore subject to recurrent drought. Where small-scale village tanks are linked to major irrigation schemes, the vulnerability to local rainfall failure is much reduced. The objective of this chapter is to analyse the vulnerability of drought-prone systems and the coping strategies adopted by the communities that farm under these systems.

A few studies have made some effort to understand the effect of drought on the livelihoods of peasant communities in Dry Zone small tank systems as well as their adjustment to drought conditions (Madduma Bandara 1982; Tennakoon 1986a, 1986b). This chapter reviews the existing evidence of household strategies for coping with drought in the Dry Zone areas and identifies a distinctive pattern of strategies, followed by a sample of drought stricken farm households in the Huruluwewa watershed of Anuradhapura District.

The effects of the 1996 drought

The failure of the north-east monsoon in the last two months of 1995, followed by the erratic behaviour of the south-east monsoon in early 1996, marked the beginning of the most recent spell of drought in the country. National statistics for 1996 indicate that nationwide crop production was seriously affected by the failure of the monsoon. The output of coconut and other food crops fell drastically in the wake of the drought. Production of the paddy crop (the mainstay of the rural economy and the main cereal consumed by the population), which recorded a peak production level in 1995, dropped drastically by 27 per cent to 2.1 million metric tons – the lowest output since 1979 (Central Bank of Sri Lanka 1996). In order to meet the shortfall in rice, the government was compelled to allow private traders to import up to 341 000 metric tons of rice in 1996 and even abolished the duties on rice imports to minimize the rice price increase. The drought also hit the industrial sector of the country. The manufacturing sector suffered badly from power cuts of up to eight hours per day imposed on consumers of electricity for nearly five months. During this drought year agricultural produce was in short supply, prices rose and the domestic market shrank as rural income fell.

Table 1. Recipients of government relief in the drought affected areas of Anuradhapura District in 1997

Divisional Secretariat Division	Percentage of population selected to receive drought relief	Percentage of families receiving Samurdhi[4] stamps	Percentage of families selected to receive drought relief	Percentage of families receiving dry food rations under the World Food Programme
Nuwaragam Palatha	59.7	37.8	65.4	1.0
Madyama Nuwagaram Palatha	7.9	57.6	8.0	1.3
Wilachchiya	10.6	66.0	17.2	3.3
Nochchiagama	9.0	60.7	14.7	4.2
Tambuththegama	12.3	28.9	9.0	–
Rajanganaya	3.1	46.6	3.0	–
Talawa	4.9	37.4	4.5	0.2
Ipalogama	3.9	61.1	8.2	0.3
Palagala	1.3	74.2	2.5	1.6
Galnewa	21.0	46.3	20.4	0.3
Kekirawa	25.5	44.9	12.2	1.6
Teroppane	9.2	29.2	11.3	2.1
Mihinthale	7.5	68.9	9.4	0.5
Kahatagasdigiliya	3.0	65.2	2.7	2.1
Horowpathana	10.8	29.3	24.7	4.2
Galenbindunuwewa	23.8	69.1	33.2	0.3
Rambewa	9.9	39.8	9.7	4.3
Medawachchiya	77.3	82.2	66.7	1.3
Kebitigollawa	10.1	63.–	38.8	3.7
Padaviya	20.1	57.4	19.1	–
Palugaswewa	8.8	23.3	8.6	–
All	20.0	52.1	20.4	1.5

Source: Department of Social Services, Kachcheri, Anuradhapura

The effect of the drought on communities depending on village tank systems in many parts of the Dry Zone was particularly severe. The districts of Kurunegala, Anuradhapura, Hambantota, Monaragala, Badulla, Ampara and Vavuniya have been identified by the Department of Social Services as those most severely affected by the drought in

---

4 *Samurdhi* is a national programme launched by the government to eliminate poverty in Sri Lanka. Benefits range from 100–1000 rupees per month, depending on the size of the family. By December 1986, 1.8 million families were benefiting from this programme. Beneficiary families leave the programme when their monthly income exceeds 2000 rupees over a continuous six-month period, or when at least one member of the family finds regular employment.

1996/97. The total number of families affected in these districts during 1996 has been estimated at 155 000 which appears to be an under-estimation. On the basis of earlier records, the district of Anuradhapura, where the small tank system dominates the landscape, was found to be one of the hardest hit and most vulnerable districts in the country.

The number of people eligible to receive drought relief in Anuradha-pura District in 1997 has been estimated by Divisional Secretaries (DSS)[5] at 36 903 families, amounting to 142 344 individuals. The population eligible to receive drought relief in the district has been estimated at 20 per cent of the total. However, there are significant variations in the percentages of families affected by drought in different Divisional Secretariat (DS) divisions across the district. For instance, over 77 per cent of the families in Medawachchiya DS division have been identified as eligible to receive drought relief (from the government, through the Department of Social Services) compared to slightly over 1 per cent of families in Palagala DS division (Table 1). Therefore the severity of drought is largely dependent upon the spatial availability of irrigation water as well as the temporal variation in rainfall within the district. The shortages of water have invariably led either to limitation of the area under crop cultivation or to complete failures of already cultivated crops in many areas.

Study area

The area for the present study was chosen from eight locations selected for the Monitoring and Evaluation (M&E) programme of the Shared Control of Natural Resources[6] (SCOR) project implemented by the International Irrigation Management Institute (IIMI) in the Huruluwewa watershed of Anuradhapura District. On the basis of the available information, Mahameegaswewa sub-watershed was selected as one of

---

5 The Divisional Secretary is the chief government adminstrative officer in an Administrative Division (there are a number of such divisions in each district), responsible to the District Secretary (formerly known as the Government Agent). Divisional Secretaries have a wide range of administrative powers.

6 Shared Control of Natural Resources (SCOR) is a participatory watershed manage-ment project aimed at developing and testing a holistic interdisciplinary approach to integrate conservation concerns with production goals. The project aims at optimizing watershed-wide land and associated water use efficiency through a package of interventions. The SCOR approach is being tested in the Huruluwewa watershed in the North Central Province (one of nine provinces in the country, each of which has two to three districts within it).

the areas severely affected by the recent drought. Mahameegaswewa is a small tank 'cascade' system[7] located in Palugaswewa DS division (Figure 1). The community of Mahameegaswewa is mainly dependent on cultivation of paddy and *chena* lands for its livelihood. The tank provides most of the water required for 17 hectares of paddy cultivation. An additional 16 hectares of highlands are cultivated by 52 households for rainfed crops. These homesteads are poorly maintained and do not generate an adequate income. Two hundred hectares of adjoining scrub jungle area are subjected to seasonal slash and burn cultivation (*chena*) by the village community.

The total number of residents living in this sub-watershed is 313 individuals belonging to 62 families. Thus the average family size is about five members. They all belong to a single caste group with close kinship ties. Mahameegaswewa is one of the most economically and socially backward villages in the Huruluwewa watershed. The economic status and living condition of the majority of the households could be considered as poor by any standard. The average household income per month for the majority of the households is below 750 rupees. Therefore, almost all families are eligible to receive food stamps[8] from the government. These food stamps were found to be the single most important source of income. This village could therefore be considered as an ideal location for the case-study.

Methodology of the study

Both secondary and primary data sources were employed in the analysis to take advantage of the strengths of both types of data and to minimize their respective weaknesses by combining them. The secondary data of this study mainly included records available in the offices of the Social Services Department at national and provincial level. However, much of the study is based upon primary data collected from a sample of 40 household heads in the Mahameegaswewa sub-watershed. This sample

---

7 A cascade system is a connected series of tanks (small reservoirs) organized within micro-catchments to store, convey and utilize water from temporary streams (Madduma Bandara 1985).

8 These are given by the government to support families living below the poverty line. The value of the stamps varies according to family size. Recipients can encash them for buying weekly provisions such as rice, grain, pulses and even kerosene. The food stamp scheme was first introduced in 1979 and has continued despite the introduction of new schemes (*Janasaviya* and *Samurdhi*) to supersede it.

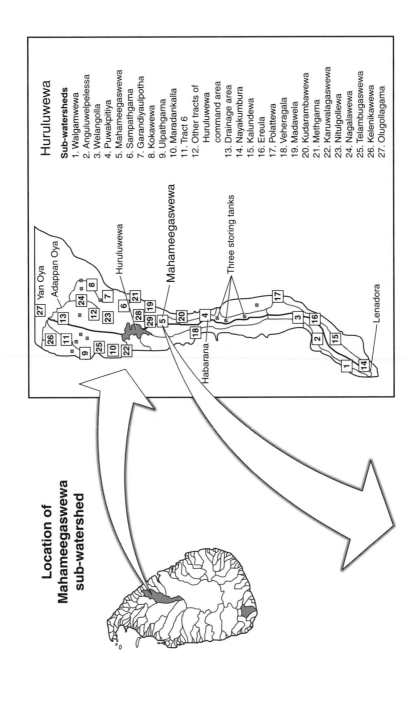

Location of Mahameegaswewa sub-watershed

Huruluwewa

Sub-watersheds
1. Walgamwewa
2. Anguluwelpelessa
3. Welangolla
4. Puwakpitiya
5. Mahameegaswewa
6. Sampathgama
7. Garandiyaulpotha
8. Kokawewa
9. Ulpathgama
10. Maradankalla
11. Tract 6
12. Other tracts of Huruluwewa command area
13. Drainage area
14. Nayakumbura
15. Kalundewa
16. Ereula
17. Polattewa
18. Veheragala
19. Madawela
20. Kudarambawewa
21. Methgama
22. Karuwalagaswewa
23. Nitulgollewa
24. Nagalawewa
25. Telambugaswewa
26. Kelenikawewa
27. Olugollagama

Yan Oya

Adappan Oya

Huruluwewa

Mahameegaswewa

Three storing tanks

Habarana

Lenadora

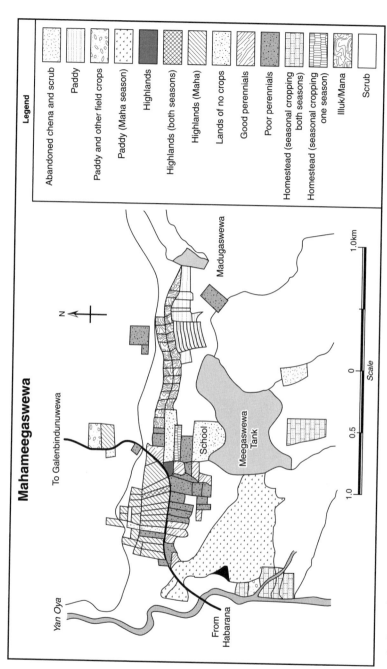

Mahameegaswewa

Legend

- Abandoned chena and scrub
- Paddy
- Paddy and other field crops
- Paddy (Maha season)
- Highlands
- Highlands (both seasons)
- Highlands (Maha)
- Lands of no crops
- Good perennials
- Poor perennials
- Homestead (seasonal cropping both seasons)
- Homestead (seasonal cropping one season)
- Illuk/Mana
- Scrub

Yan Oya

To Galenbindunuwewa

From Habarana

School

Meegaswewa Tank

Madugaswewa

N

Scale

0.5 0 0.5 1.0 1.0km

Figure 1. Location of Mahameegaswewa sub-watershed

amounts to nearly 65 per cent of the total household heads. The collection of micro-level data comprised structured in-depth interviews with a sample of individuals, and unstructured group interviews with key informants. The participatory observation method was employed for the collection of qualitative data during the previous one-and-a-half year period by the data collector assigned to this area under the SCOR M&E programme. This method comprises sharing in the life and activities of the community, observing, and supplementing the knowledge by conversation and interviews. A series of focus group interviews was conducted by the author in order to obtain supplementary information on the theme from residents in the study location. This was a part of the strategy of collecting data by the group interview method.

The field data collection, using structured questionnaires on the specific themes of drought and coping strategies, was carried out during the month of July 1997 by the resident data collector in Mahameegaswewa. This period usually represents the water-deficient *Yala*[9] season in the Dry Zone. No cultivation was possible in the study area during the 1997 *Yala* season. The previous *Maha*[10] season had also been affected by the inadequate rainfall. Although 43 per cent of farmers had cultivated paddy during the 1996 *Yala* season, the crop was completely damaged by the prevailing drought. The farmers were able to cultivate only a few crops on their *chena* lands during the 1996/97 *Maha* season, which was also severely affected by the drought. Therefore, the period from 1996 up to the time of our survey can be considered in many ways as a typical 'drought' for the residents of Mahameegaswewa.

Farmers' perceptions of drought

Farmers' perception of the condition of drought is reported to be influenced by a number of factors. As shown by Tennakoon (1986b), it is influenced by the impact of water shortages on one's vital interest, past experiences of working and living in abundant or low rainfall areas, the perceived advantage of one's place of living, varying aridity in a given

9 The south-west monsoon which coincides with the *Yala* season (from late May to late September) brings less rain to the Dry Zone. Paddy cultivation in the Dry Zone areas during *Yala* is dependent upon the availability of supplementary irrigation facilities as the rainfall is insufficient to cultivate rainfed paddy. Therefore *Yala* is the minor season in the Dry Zone.

10 *Maha* is the major crop season which receives much of the rainfall from the north-east monsoon (from November to February) in the Dry Zone.

geographical area, the frequency of drought occurrence, and the magnitude of the drought.

Perceptions of the drought among Mahameegaswewa farmers appear to be remarkably similar. The major characteristic of the drought as perceived by the majority of the respondents (95 per cent) was inadequate rainfall to undertake paddy cultivation during the *Maha* season. The inability to cultivate paddy or other seasonal crops during the *Yala* season was considered normal by all of them. The shortage of drinking water (45 per cent of respondents), lack of water and food for animals plus inability to provide sufficient food for households (28 per cent) were considered to be extreme conditions of a drought. The respondents' perception of the frequency of drought, on the basis of their past experiences, also indicated remarkable similarities. The majority of the farmers (73 per cent) indicated that drought occurred in a three-year cycle. The others indicated drought as a more frequent phenomenon, possibly due to the unusual length of the current drought.

The respondents were requested to name the most recent drought years on the basis of severity (defined in terms of the magnitude of crop losses, length of dry period and the reduction in the availability of food reserves). Forty per cent of the households (heads of household) considered the 1995–96 period as having had the most devastating effect on the economy of households, while 60 per cent considered the effect of drought was more severe on them during 1996–97. Overall, 88 per cent of the households indicated that they were very vulnerable to the drought and the recent drought had been particularly severe on them. The remaining households (12 per cent) stated that the effects on them had been moderate. Household vulnerability to drought therefore appears to have varied considerably depending on the economic standing of each household.

The effect of drought on land use patterns

As in many other village tank systems in the Dry Zone of Sri Lanka, the main economic activities of the people living in Mahameegaswewa are rainfed and irrigated farming along with maintaining a limited stock of livestock. The different types of land owned by families interviewed are given in Table 2.

According to Table 2, 12.5 per cent of the households did not own any paddy lands. The majority of the households owned paddy allotments of less than 0.5 hectares. The average holding size of paddy was

Table 2. Percentage of households owning agricultural land in Mahameegaswewa during the 1996/97 Maha season

Category	Paddy Land		High Land		Chena Land*	
Land size (hectares)	% of Households	Total Extent (hectares)	% of Households	Total Extent (hectares)	% of Households	Total Extent (hectares)
no landholding	12.5	–	–	–	37.5	–
< 0.25	25	1.54	17.5	1.44	5	0.41
0.26–0.50	25	3.79	57.5	9.33	12.5	2.05
0.51–0.75	22.5	5.33	12.5	3.07	32.5	6.77
> 0.76	15	6.15	12.5	4.51	12.5	5.3
Total	100	16.81	100	18.35	100	14.36
N = 40						
Average size	–	0.47	–	0.46	–	0.57

* Cultivated extent of *Chena* Land
Source: Household Survey 1997

0.47 hectares. All households owned a highland homestead with an average holding size of 0.46 hectares. *Chena* land was cultivated by only 63 per cent of the households, with the average holding size being relatively large (0.57 hectares).

Paddy was cultivated in the low lying area below the Mahameegaswewa tank. The most recent successful year of paddy cultivation was the 1994/95 *Maha* season. The total area under paddy cultivation in that season was 17 hectares and the average paddy yield reported was 4.22 metric tons/hectare or 85 bushels/hectare (Hemakumara *et al*. undated). Although paddy (5.71 hectares) and chillies (0.92 hectares) were cultivated with tank water during the 1995 *Yala* season, they were severely affected by the lack of irrigation water at critical periods of crop growth. The reported yield was very low, amounting to only 1.43 metric tons/hectare of paddy and 0.461 metric tons/hectare of chillies. The poor water availability continued to affect the paddy crop in the 1995/96 *Maha* season: the average yield realized was only 2.7 metric tons/hectare for paddy. Although 48 per cent of the households cultivated their paddy land during the 1996 *Yala* season, none of them was able to reap the harvest. No crop had been cultivated under the Mahameegaswewa tank either in the 1996/97 *Maha* or 1997 *Yala* seasons. Unless above-average rainfall is received in the *Maha* season to fill the dried-up tank, it is absolutely impossible to cultivate paddy during the following *Yala* season.

The rainfall fluctuations have also affected average yields by leading to the adoption by paddy farmers of poor management practices such as dry sowing, poor weeding, low levels of fertilizer application and inadequate disease and pest control. The weather failures had discouraged them from using costly inputs or adopting expensive management practices.

Homesteads or home gardens can be defined as either a permanent or semi-permanent system of highland farming. Annual and semi-permanent crops or permanent tree crops dominate the homesteads which are characterized by clearly demarcated land allotments with 'live fences' (of plants, bushes, trees) at the boundaries. All the farmers in the sample possess homesteads and their dwellings are located in these highlands. The most popular semi-permanent or permanent crops grown in the homesteads of Mahameegaswewa are lime, mango, coconut, drumstick (*Moringa Oleifera*: a common tree crop grown in live fences), jackfruit and some valuable timber species such as teak and margosa (*neem*). Most of these tree crops are considered to be drought tolerant. The cropping practices found in home gardens are highly disorganized except in a few homesteads where interventions have been made under the SCOR project. Even in those cases farmers have not been able to raise seasonal crops due to the depletion of moisture levels in the wake of the prolonged drought. Hence, the income that could be derived from tree crops in homegardens was negligible at the time of crisis. As found elsewhere in areas served by small tank systems in the district, farmers in the study area paid less attention to their homesteads than to their other landholdings and left the homestead in the care of their children and wives (Madduma Bandara 1982: 53).

The farmers in Mahameegaswewa were successful only in raising a small area of crops on their *chena* lands during the 1996/97 *Maha* season, as a number of subsidiary crops thrive under conditions of moisture stress. The main crops cultivated by farmers in their *chena* lands included maize, chilli, cowpea, black gram, pumpkin and a variety of mixed vegetable crops. However, the uncertainty of rainfall prevented a substantial number of farmers from investing their meagre resources in the risky cultivation of *chena*. As revealed in the field survey, only 63 per cent (25 households) of the total sample households cultivated *chena* land during the 1996/97 *Maha* season despite the fact that there was no limitation on the accessibility of *chena* land in the vicinity. Of the 25 households who did cultivate *chena*, 14 (56 per cent) reported partial crop failures as a result of unfavourable weather. Their maize crop was stunted due to lack of rainfall at critical stages of crop growth, resulting in poor output. The chilli crop suffered not only from lack of water but also from a slump in price in the open market.[11] All categories of land user therefore suffered from the prevailing drought conditions or other external factors.

Ninety-five per cent of the households stated that their agricultural income had fallen during the reference period and some 80 per cent complained of increased indebtedness. The drought has also had a long-lasting effect on nutritional deficiencies and related diseases and the weakening of labour quality among household members. Thirty per cent

---

11 Chilli farmers were not able to market their produce due to the flooding of the local market by cheap imported chillies at the time of harvest. There was a series of public protests and extensive media coverage of the government's open door policy on imports of agricultural commodities that could be produced locally.

of the households mentioned an increased incidence of family illness during the 1996–97 drought.

Household coping strategies

Adjustments to the drought by Dry Zone communities have been analysed by several authors with reference to previous major droughts in 1974–77 and 1981–82 (Madduma Bandara 1982; Tennakoon 1986a, 1986b). Madduma Bandara has analysed adjustment to the 1981 drought among a sample of 483 families drawn from 49 *purana* (traditional) villages in Mahapotana *korale*.[12] Tennakoon (1986a, 1986b) studied three traditional villages and two colonization schemes (Wilachchiya and Rajangana) in Anuradhapura District with regard to household adjustment to the 1974–77 drought. In a subsequent study he analysed adjustment by settlers to the 1981–82 drought in system H of the Mahaweli Development Area.

Based on his field studies, Tennakoon identifies two major types of adjustment among drought-affected farmers:

1. adjustment which affects the basic cause of hazards
2. adjustments in the form of sharing and suffering.

Under the first type of adjustment, farmers turn towards supernatural powers to avoid the occurrence of drought or to curb it when it is in progress. Actions include vowing to hold ceremonial alms-giving, holding ceremonies and making offerings to please the guardian gods of the village in anticipation of timely rain. However, none of the farmers in Mahameegaswewa resorted to similar activities during the recent drought period.

Adjustment in the form of sharing and suffering was widely adopted by the sample of farmers studied by both Tennakoon and Madduma Bandara. Tennakoon (1986b) identified 26 adjustments, which can be grouped under the following main headings:

o food rations, relief payment and assistance
o use of previous food reserves
o borrowing
o income from non-agricultural employment

---

12 A *korale*, consisting of a large number of villages, was an administrative unit in the colonial period.

o reduce expenditure
o food gathering
o mortgage and sale.

During the course of our field survey in Mahameegaswewa, respondents were asked to identify what remedial measures were taken by them to overcome the hardships created by the drought. Table 3 summarizes the range of strategies adopted by households. The rank given in the table indicates the relative significance of commonly adopted strategies based on the percentage of households adopting them. The sequential importance of the strategy is indicated by stage.

The purchase of foods on credit from traders was the most commonly adopted strategy (however, in most villages this seems to be possible mainly for the more credit-worthy farmers). Food stamps provided by the government constituted the most important source of income for 85 per cent of the households. The main strategy adopted by the households studied by Madduma Bandara in Mahapotana *korale* at the time of the 1981 drought was cutting down on meals. Only 35 per cent of households in Mahameegaswewa cut down the number of meals per day; but 75 per cent of the households reduced the variety and quality of food consumed. It was revealed during the focus group interviews that the majority of households had not been able to consume the average three meals of rice per day. The midday meal (if not skipped) was substituted by corn, cowpea, yam or bread. Cutting down on meals may have been underestimated by respondents as there was general reluctance to reveal to an outsider that they had to endure hunger at times of crisis. The only way of supplementing household income during drought periods was wage labouring within and outside the village – including a variety of activities in production and services. Table 3 shows a substantial number of households supplementing their income in this manner.

As far as the stages of adopting various coping strategies are concerned, it is important to note that the risk of food insecurity was anticipated and household strategies were carefully planned accordingly. The strategies listed under stage 1 in Table 3 were adopted at the early stages of drought and those listed under stage 2 followed later, particularly when the food crisis deepened.

The first stage strategies began by looking for alternative sources of income which did not disturb the subsistence base of the household. Later on during the first stage, households introduced austerity measures

Table 3. Coping strategies followed by sample households

	% H/holds	Rank	Stage
Food rations, relief payment and assistance →			1
○ food stamps provided by the government	85	2	
○ dry rations received for working under the Participatory Forestry Programme (PFP)	43	9	
○ remittances received from children in paid employment	8	15	
Use of reserves →			2
○ reserves of seed paddy	63	7	
○ past cash savings	78	3	
Borrowing/exchanges →			1
○ exchange food with neighbours	73	5	
○ purchase foodstuff on credit from traders	90	1	
○ obtain credit at high interest rate from traders/money lenders	18	14	
Income from off-farm activities →			1
○ work as casual labourers within village	65	6	
○ work as casual labourers outside village	45	8	
○ engage in non-farm activities	23	12	
Reduce expenditure →			1
○ postponement of special functions (marriages, engagement, etc.)	10	16	
○ celebration of important festivals with less entertainment	65	6	
○ reduction in variety and quality of foods consumed	75	4	
○ reduction of number of meals per day	33	10	
Mortgages and sales →			2
○ mortgage personal effects (e.g. jewellery and household goods)	30	11	
○ sale of personal effects, household goods, implements	20	13	
○ sale of cattle	10	16	
Change of cropping strategies →			1
○ cultivate land outside the village	13	15	
○ cultivate land from wells/pumps	5	17	
Migration →			1
○ temporary migration to other areas for employment	33	10	
N = 40			

Source: Household Survey 1997.

such as reduction in the variety and quality of food or in the number of meals per day. At the same time, increased reliance was placed on credit and exchange of foods within and between households. Temporary migration for employment took place in the latter part of this stage.

When all these avenues were exhausted households turned to the second stage, which involved disposal of productive assets by way of sales or mortgage: this necessarily disturbed the capital base of the household. In such circumstances the household's ability to generate current or future income was severely weakened. Overall, fewer households adopted second stage strategies than first stage strategies. The austerity measures were the most popular form of coping strategies adopted by the majority of the households in the sample.

As drought is a regular occurrence in the Dry Zone, the response of resource-poor farming families is carefully structured. Our field survey and observations show that individuals implement increasingly severe austerity measures as drought progresses – ultimately disposing of assets.

Drought relief policies

The provision of drought relief goes back to the colonial period. The usual practice has been for the Government Agent (District Secretary) to send instructions to the Assistant Government Agents (Divisional Secretaries) to select eligible families to receive relief on the recommendation of the village-level officers (*Grama Niladhari*). The total number of drought affected families in Sri Lanka and the total amount of aid paid during 1981–97 is given in Table 4. These official figures do not necessarily indicate the full extent of the problem. The previous method of paying drought relief in the form of food stamps and cash payment was changed in 1996. According to the new government circular No.96/3 on drought relief payment, recipients should satisfy the following conditions to be eligible to receive cash payments as drought relief:

o the monthly income of the recipient family should be less than 2000 rupees and this should be derived from agriculture or related activities
o cultivation of seasonal crops should have been disrupted or damaged for at least two consecutive seasons due to drought
o lack of any alternative source of income for the family other than agriculture or related activities

o the agricultural crops of the recipient family should not be covered by any insurance scheme

o the beneficiaries of the *Samurdhi* programme are not included in the drought relief programme, as the government pays them relief through an alternative scheme.

During the period in receipt of relief, at least one member of the recipient family is required to work a minimum of 12 days per month on work sites initiated to create community assets such as roads, minor irrigation tanks and channels, and conservation-related earthworks in order to increase the productive capacity of dryland agriculture in subsequent years. The amount of aid given is dependent upon the number of members in the target families. For example, a single-member family is eligible to receive 50 rupees per day with a maximum of 600 rupees per month. A two-member family is eligible to receive a maximum of 1200 rupees per month.

However, none of the sample households in Mahameegaswewa benefited from the drought relief programme during 1996–97. Ninety-five per cent of the households are recipients of *Samurdhi* benefits: therefore they have not been included as beneficiaries of the drought relief programme. Nevertheless, under the special direction of the President,

Table 4. Number of drought-affected families and drought relief payments in Sri Lanka 1981–97

Year	Number of Affected Families	Total Amount of Aid Paid (Rs.)
1981	204 211	42 654 647
1982	372 436	118 920 957
1983	435 926	87 929 636
1984	3008	209 842
1985	20 498	4 886 513
1986	5303	480 845
1987	484 925	72 969 136
1988	652 363	28 553 911
1989	238 420	24 335 145
1990	203 794	6 721 942
1991	203 794	230 202 076
1996	155 006	424 855 387
1997	88 286	85 655 740

Note: No relief payments were made during the period 1992–95
Source: Department of Social Services

Samurdhi recipients in some areas in the district were given partial payment of drought relief in 1996–97.

The government's drought relief programme has often been criticized as liberal (i.e. given to the undeserving) and ineffective. The programme has also often been abused by the officials. Another criticism leveled against the programme was that the type of work undertaken has made a minimal contribution to minimizing the effect of drought damage in the long run (Madduma Bandara 1982). The other comment often made against this programme is that relief policies directed at protection of consumption are very often made operative only when the farmers resort to disposal of productive assets. Therefore the relief policies also appear to ignore the sequence of farmers' adjustment mechanisms.

Alternative strategies promoted by the SCOR project in Mahameegaswewa

Mahameegaswewa was one of the sub-watersheds selected by the SCOR project for implementation of a package of interventions aimed at enhancing the capacity of households to resist natural calamities in future. The package was formulated jointly by professionals and resource users in 1994. The range of intervention strategies followed in the Mahameegaswewa sub-watershed can be summarized under the following headings:

o stabilization of *chena* and 'encroached' lands (government land occupied without authorization)
o regeneration of the eco-system associated with the tanks (i.e. catchment area, water/tank bed drainage system and the immediate settlements)
o integrated management of land and water resources
o sharing resources for improving homesteads
o consolidation of fragmented land holdings below the minor tanks to form viable economic units.

Following a participatory planning exercise, a 'mini-project' was formulated for implementation with an investment of 1.2 million rupees (US$ 24 000). This mini-project sought to enable changes in land and water management strategies in the Mahameegaswewa area through promotion of diversification of crops and introduction of improved conservation practices. Specific interventions include:

- promotion of water-saving practices to enable more intensive cropping
- introduction of fast-maturing commercial crops in the dry season
- cultivation of medicinal plants, fruits and drought-resistant timber species in *chena* and homestead areas
- stabilized cropping systems in *chena* lands and highlands[13]
- improved highland cultivation practices including contour bunds, mulching, water harvesting and green manuring
- improved livestock husbandry
- community forestry. (Wijayaratne 1996)

The SCOR interventions are designed to provide short-, medium- and long-term benefits to the community. In the short term improved land and water management should increase seasonal yields; in the medium term improvement of soil conditions will increase resilience to droughts; in the long term increased productivity of fruits and timber will further reduce the communities' reliance on seasonal crop production. However, the severity of the 1996 drought has severely constrained the implementation of the proposed interventions and has restricted the benefits to the local community.

Conclusion

Households faced with considerable threats to their food requirements as a result of drought adopt a range of responses to minimize the impact. The particular response followed by households tends to have a clear pattern which can be interpreted in terms of the economic standing of each household. The sequence of responses followed by them suggests that their primary concern is to avoid disturbing the future income-earning capacity of the household. Hence, each household resorts to austerity measures that have the minimum impact on its economic base.

The present state policies of bringing relief to the affected families were found to be largely ineffective. It is imperative to direct future policies towards minimizing household vulnerability to drought rather than bringing relief to the households once they are affected.

---

13 Shifting cultivation was common in the Dry Zone highlands in the past. In recent years, the fallow period has been shortened due to greater demand for land (an outcome of population growth). The establishment of stabilized cropping practices is a priority for agricultural planning in the Dry Zone.

Adoption of more sustainable land use patterns giving due consideration to increasing production and protecting the environment has been identified as a testable option which could minimize the impact of drought. The diversification of households' income-earning opportunities is a viable option which would lower the risk arising from their sole dependency on land.

4. Coping with Climatic Disasters in Isolated Hill Communities of Nepal: the Case of Rampur Village in Okhaldhunga

NGAMINDRA DAHAL

Introduction

PEOPLE LIVING IN the Himalayan region cope with the uncertain climate and its extremes. Concentrated rain, hailstorms, thunderstorms and drought are common. Such events often lead to landslides, floods, famine or starvation and water scarcity. People have developed skills to cope with such disasters. In many cases, communities affected by disasters survive the hardships; they rehabilitate their houses, terraces and natural resource base – a task which may continue for several years after the disaster. In the course of rehabilitation and struggle for survival, many cannot cope and are forced to abandon their ancestral homes. Others continue as long as they are able to do so.

Cloudbursts and their impact

Cloudbursts[1] are frequent in the region but forecasting them is beyond current capacity, for economic and technical reasons.[2] A single cloudburst

---

1 A cloudburst is one of the three extreme rainfall events: the other two are monsoon depression and tropical cyclone. Generally speaking, cloudbursts are associated with thunderstorms and occur most often in desert and mountain regions, and in the interiors of continents. The uprushing air currents of thunderstorms support a large amount of water (in the form of raindrops). If the air currents are suddenly cut off, the mass of rain falls quickly over a small area. Some meteorologists categorize cloudbursts as events with rainfall of 100 millimetres per hour or more.

2 Forecasting is not impossible technically but it requires continuous monitoring of surrounding climatic activities which include the rain-bearing nature, movements and thickness of clouds, wind and temperature profiles at surface and upper levels, and topographical features of the area concerned. Such continuous monitoring is possible only with the use of sophisticated instruments such as radar and automatic data recording and processing computers. This technology, however, has yet to be tested in mountain regions. Besides the installation and operating costs, forecasting extreme weather events such as cloudbursts is still a challenge because of the short time span in which they occur.

47

can become catastrophic when a community is hit, leading in some cases to loss of life and property. In Nepal, high intensity rainfall triggers floods (the local term is *badhi*) and landslides (*pahiro*) from the upper slopes, bringing down boulders and debris flows.

Nepal is frequently affected by cloudbursts in the rainy monsoon period (June to September). People in the mountain region[3] are the major sufferers.[4] There is hardly any community in the hills which has not had at least one person killed or maimed by landslides and floods in living memory. In some villages such events strike in an inevitable but unpredictable fashion, leaving one or two decades of quiescence. In other villages, they are more frequent.

The main natural reasons for these disasters, in addition to the torrential rain, are the tectonic instability of the region, the steepness of the terrain and the fact that the Himalaya is a geologically young mountain range which is still unstable (DPTC 1993). In recent times there has been an increase in human settlement and cultivation, even in hazard-prone zones. People displaced by earlier disasters also live in such regions. As a result, more and more people are vulnerable to natural disaster. The annual loss of life and property from floods and landslides is given in Table 1.

The cloudbursts in Nepal in 1993 were unusually powerful and destructive. There were two major events. One was a series of several cloudbursts in the watershed zone of the Bagmati River, the major river of central Nepal, from 19 to 22 July, which caused general destruction in the mountain as well as in the Terai (plains) region. The earlier event that occurred in the first week of July was localized and hit villages in Okhaldhunga District in the eastern hills. This chapter uses this earlier event as a case-study.

Rampur village

Rampur is a village of about three square kilometres in area in Baruneswor Village Development Committee (VDC) which comprises

---

3 Nepal is divided into three principal geographic-ecological zones: the southern plains (at varying heights between 60 and 1000 metres above sea level), the middle hills (generally 400 to 3000 metres above sea level) and the mountains (from 2500 metres to the high Himalayan peaks).

4 It has been estimated that the average rate of soil loss in Nepal's mountains is 20 to 50 tons/hectare/year, but in severely eroded areas the rate can be as high as 200 to 500 tons/hectare/year (Laban 1978).

48

Table 1. Loss of life and property caused by floods and landslides in Nepal

Year	Number of deaths	Number of livestock killed	Number of houses destroyed or damaged	Affected land (hectares)
1983	293	284	–	–
1985	420	3056	4620	13 544
1987	391	1438	33 721	188 597
1989	680	1512	6024	–
1990	307	314	3060	1132
1991	93	36	817	283
1992	71	179	88	135
1993	1336	25 424	17 113	5584
1994	49	284	569	392
1995	246	1935	5162	41 867

Sources: Deshantar 1993; DPTC 1996

several villages in in Okhaldhunga District.[5] It is one of 56 VDCs in the district, which lies in the middle hill region of Nepal.

There are 5500 people living in Baruneswor VDC. The majority of the population is from the two upper castes, *Brahmin* and *Chhetri*. The rest are of (lower) occupational castes such as *Damai*, (tailor), *Sarki* (shoemaker) and *Kami* (blacksmith). There are more than 10 cluster settlements at different places in the VDC. It is estimated that about 50 per cent of the VDC's population live in Rampur.

A higher secondary school, health post, area post office, two water mills and a recently installed VHF (very high frequency) telephone set are the few modern amenities in the village. Piped drinking water systems have also been built. Sale depots for chemical fertilizers and seeds and a forest nursery are run by the Sajha Co-operatives (a public co-operative programme promoted by the government, which raises funds by selling shares to local farmers and entrepreneurs and investing the funds in beneficial activities chosen by the shareholders). Irrigation is based on farmer-built canals. A weekly market is another local feature. There is no electricity; people use kerosene lamps for light in the evening.

Okhaldhunga District is not reached by any motorable road. Rampur

---

5 The socio-economic information that follows was collected by the author from a field survey. Population figures for Baruneswor VDC were supplied by the Central Bureau of Statistics.

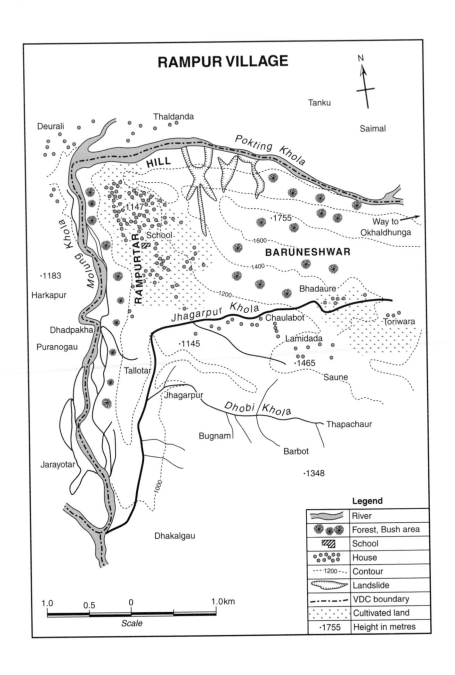

RAMPUR VILLAGE

N

Tanku

Deurali   Thaldanda   Saimal

Pokting Khola

HILL

Way to
Okhaldhunga

·1147   School   ·1755

·1600

BARUNESHWAR

Kholang Molung Khola

·1400

·1183   ·1200

Harkapur   Bhadaure

Jhagarpur Khola   Chaulabot   Toriwara

Dhadpakha   Lamidada

Puranogau   ·1145

·1465

Tallotar   Saune

Jhagarpur

Dhobi Khola

Thapachaur

Bugnam

Barbot

Jarayotar

·1348

·1000

Dhakalgau

Legend

	River
	Forest, Bush area
	School
	House
---·1200·---	Contour
	Landslide
—·—·—	VDC boundary
	Cultivated land
·1755	Height in metres

1.0   0.5   0   1.0km

Scale

is three hours walking distance (about eight kilometres) west from the district headquarters. The nearest point linked by road is Katari Bazaar in Udayapur District which is two days walking distance (about 100 kilometres) south of Rampur. There is an airport at Rumjatar, five kilometres south-east of Okhaldhunga District headquarters. Sick people are carried on the back of a porter to get to hospital.

Topographical features

The village is situated at a height of 1147 metres above sea level on a flat river terrace which is locally called a *tar*. The *tar* is a plateau-like land form with a reddish soil on the surface rising to a height of 500 metres from the Molung River, a snow-fed river that flows along the west and south sides of the village. The river that flanks the village to the east is the Jhagarpur *Khola*.[6]

Immediately to the north of the village rises a large hill or mountain that is elongated in an east-west direction, rising in the west from the Molung River and extending east of Rampur. From north to south it ranges between 50 and 200 metres in breadth. Its elevation (above sea level) is 1500 metres at its western end and 2000 metres at its peak some three kilometres to the east: for these three kilometres it forms the northern frontier of the village, after which it curves northwards. At the top it is narrow and covered with pine trees and boulders of different sizes. It serves as the source of drinking water, fodder and forest products for the villagers. The mountain experiences small and moderate landslides. The Pokting River – a major tributary of the Molung – flows along the bottom of the northern side of the mountain. Rampur is therefore virtually surrounded by large and small rivers in three directions: east, west and south.

The mountain is composed of carbonaceous fragmentary rocks. The soil texture ranges from clay to gravel. Boulders of various sizes are also found. The uplands soil is colluvial or partly colluvial in character. The unconsolidated mass of colluvial deposits is prone to failure, while residual soils suffer from surface erosion. Landslides occur frequently in the terraced farmland downstream. The mountain of Rampur is unstable at different sections due to its steep slope, unconsolidated structure and destabilized old landslides.

Only the western part of Rampur is relatively safe from floods and

---

6 *Khola* is the usual Nepali term for river but tends to indicate relatively small or seasonal river channels.

landslides. This is so because, first, at this point the mountain to the north is relatively low; and second, the slope here is stable and covered with forest.

The slope of the mountain north of the centre of the village (the settlement zone and adjacent farmland) is formed by an old landslide. Grassland and bushy forest have covered part of the slope, whereas the rest is wasteland. East of this there is no settlement. The upper section is forested while the lower sections are cultivated in the form of bench terraces. The west and south of Rampur *tar* is cultivated. The landscape of the village is slightly tilted towards the Jhagarpur *Khola* in the east and south-east.

The climate in Rampur is pleasant. Because of the rugged topography, which consists of deep river gorges and mountain chain, temperature and other climatic factors vary within a short distance. There is no climatic station in Rampur. The nearest one is at the district head-quarters about eight kilometres away. There was no accurate measure-ment of the cloudburst that led to the 1993 disaster. Okhaldhunga District receives 1960 millimetres of rainfall in a year, on average.

However, Rampur faces an acute shortage of water for drinking and irrigation for seven months (November to May) every year. The Jhagarpur *Khola* that irrigates two-thirds of the village during the mon-soon becomes dry in these months. The Molung River is not useful to the village because it flows at a lower elevation than the Rampur *tar* and is suitable only for the irrigation of the paddy field on its bank. Conse-quently the village has a poor economic base despite its productive soil and favourable climate.

A canal was built by the government but works only seasonally. It is four kilometres long from Pokting River to Rampur. It was completed in 1987 after 10 years of construction. The canal, which was one of largest projects in Okhaldhunga, collapsed within three weeks of coming into operation. The government then abandoned it but later local people themselves brought it back into operation after several months of volunteer labour, using local construction materials (e.g. stone, brush-wood and mud). About one kilometre of the canal passes through the active landslide zone of the steep mountain slope.

After each monsoon, sections of the canal slide down the mountain-side and the villagers rehabilitate the canal, with considerable effort, to bring water to the village to cope with the acute shortage of water in the dry months. However, in some years their efforts do not bear fruit because of the severity of the damage. After the flood of July 1993 it was two years before they rehabilitated the canal, with the help of the District Development Committee.

Features of the landslide zone

A map of geologically hazardous areas of Nepal prepared by Dikshit (1990) shows Okhaldhunga District to be in a 'high landslide hazard zone'. Of 75 districts in the country, seven districts including Okhaldhunga are categorized as 'very poor' in terms of watershed conditions. The three kilometre long hill to the north of Rampur *tar* is geophysically fragile.

The slope from the central to the eastern part of the hill was shaped by a major landslide in the past. Old people in Rampur who know about its history tell the story about the *tera salko badhi*[7] of 1856 when a large chunk of land mass, about one kilometre long, slipped to the foot of the mountain and changed the shape of the village into the present form. Since that time, according to them, villagers have shifted to settle in the western and southern part of the village. Today, the dense settlement is still in the west and has only gradually expanded to the east. After the major landslide in 1856, there were slope falls in the central part while the rest of the area turned into dense forest. People developed bench terraces as fertile fields in the downstream area.

Each of the landslides that has occurred in Rampur has had its origin at or near the top of the hill slope. During heavy precipitation, when a moderate landslide is triggered in a flood gully on the upstream mountain slope, the landslide and water current gradually increase and turn into a debris flow. Trees, boulders and loose rocks along the bed are washed down. The debris flow accelerates as it comes down. On the way downstream some of the landslides split into two or more branches. Finally, most of them end at the Jhagarpur *Khola* at the east and southeast of the village. Their lengths range between one and three kilometres, and the maximum breadth is 500 metres.

Agricultural economy

The first or second major source of income of 99 per cent of the population of Rampur is agriculture. The products are mainly consumed within the village and only a few families are able to export surplus food

---

7 Literally, the 'flood of the year 13' – that is, the year 1913 in the Bikram Era or 1856 AD.

regularly. A weekly *haat bazaar* (market fair) is the major event for marketing their products. The majority of exchanges are still in materials, although it has significantly changed from material to cash forms in the last few years.

The major items brought to the market for sale by villagers are rice, millet, maize, vegetables, fruits and ghee. They buy clothes, kerosene, salt, soap, sugar, utensils, etc. from the market. Katari Bazaar in Udayapur District in the south is the nearest motorable road to Rampur. A porter carrying loads takes three to four days to reach Rampur from Katari. The price of each item brought from Katari is almost doubled in Rampur. For example, one kilogram of salt costs four rupees at Katari and seven to nine rupees at Rampur.

The gentle slope and flat landscape features of Rampur have made it an attractive place for agriculture and settlement. This is one of the few attractive locations in the entire hilly region, which is characterized by deep gorges of rivers, valleys and rugged mountains. However, owing to the lack of irrigation, except in the monsoon, the place is no different in its crop production from other villages in the surrounding hills.

Agricultural work (including animal husbandry) and household activities are heavily dependent on women. The majority of men are involved at the time of paddy planting (July) and harvesting (November).

Table 2. Seasonal cropping pattern in Rampur

Months	Climate		Major types of crop	
	Season	Characteristics	khet *(terraces)*	bari *(slopes)*
June–September	Monsoon	Abundant rainfall. Hot days in river valley (*besi*).	Paddy. Maize ready to harvest.	Millet, buckwheat, cereals. Maize ready to harvest.
October	Post-monsoon	Usually no rain, calm and pleasant weather	Paddy ready to harvest	Millet, cereals, green vegetables
November–February	Winter	Cold, moderate rain	Wheat and rice where irrigation is available	Dry and bare of crops; or mustard
March–May	Pre-monsoon	Intermittent rainfall with hailstorms, wind thunderstorms and dry for several weeks	Maize. Wheat ready to harvest	Maize

54

Usually men and women engage in their duties as defined traditionally. Women are required to look after all household chores such as cooking, cleaning, grinding, collecting fodder and firewood and regular monitoring of farmland and the condition of crops. For this they get up as early as four o'clock in the morning (before dawn) and go to bed late at night after completing all the work, when their male partners and children are already asleep.

Men are ususally responsible for carrying out heavy work such as the construction and maintenance of canals and terraces, climbing trees for fodder, carrying loads and ploughing fields (*hali kam*). During the *ropain* (rice planting work), men prepare fields by ploughing, leveling, and repairing terrace sides and canals for irrigating fields, while women plant rice in them. Women receive lower wages than their male partners. The difference varies depending on the nature of the work.

Non-agricultural economic activities

Although agriculture is the villagers' major source of income, sale of surplus food produce is not enough to purchase their basic needs (for salt, kerosene oil, clothes, sugar, medicine, etc.). For this reason, people are always looking for alternative source of income; long-standing debts transferred from former generations, low productivity, and shortage of food due to drought and flood are other factors behind this.

Agriculture, service, daily labour (*khetala*), business, portering and seasonal migration to the city are among the major areas of employment (see Table 3). One or more members of each family may be involved in any one or two of these fields, which generates cash income.

Land management in the monsoon

Farmers understand the importance of monsoon rains and conservation of land resources. They use several techniques to mitigate the effects of floods from the upstream mountains and at the same time they trap the floods for irrigation and conserve water for the next dry season. If there are no landslides, floods of water do not become a major problem.

Soil loss in the form of landslides and erosion is the major problem faced in the mountains. Water (in the form of rain, surface flow and underground flow) acts as the major agent in causing soil loss. In Rampur, water is abundant only during the rainy days of the monsoon. At other times water shortage is evident. In this context, villagers for

Table 3. Alternative income sources for villagers

Source of employment	Type of work or employment	Type of person employed
Teaching at schools	Government job	High school graduate or more educated person (mainly male)
Business	Local shop to sell imported goods	Families that have migrated to the village
khetala	Work on farmlands (daily wages)	Mainly women from economically backward or landless families
hali	Ploughing fields by oxen (annual contract basis)	Males from backward or landless families
Portering	Carrying loads; usually from Katari to Rampur (seasonal)	Majority are male
lahure*/migration to city	Army service, helper or guard of business houses in India (lahure)/ work of any kind	Adult male/youth
Others (legal assistant, religious work, etc.)	Assist villagers in need and get fees	Male

* In the past, many middle class youths used to leave the village with the aim of joining the British or Indian army and those who failed in this worked as helpers, guards, etc. When they return home with money and goods, they are called *lahure*. At present this does not happen in Rampur.

decades have taken measures to conserve monsoon water by making a network of ponds so that water from different sources flows into them; water released from upstream passes to the next pond downstream. Small outlets in between allow the flow of water into the vegetable gardens of nearby households. These man-made ponds are useful for three different purposes:

○ run-off management
○ water conservation
○ soil/nutrients/organic matter conservation.

It is the general tendency of all farmers to convert their slope land (*bari*) into level terraces (*khet*). Every year the area of *khet* is increasing. The price of *khet* land is much higher than *bari*. The principal benefit of the

56

khet is paddy cultivation. In *bari* only millet and maize types can be grown; soil and fertilizer loss is also very high. Although the benefits from *khet* are greater, it is highly labour consuming and expensive to convert *bari* into *khet*. Farmers are equally aware of the fact that unless there is irrigation or enough water during the period of paddy cultivation, there will be a disastrous effect on the land, along with the crops, with the surface cracking into many pieces. Therefore, terrace leveling is not possible everywhere.

Slopes are stabilized by employing different measures, including stoneworks. These types of measure are used mainly in canal protection and terrace walls. Stoneworks are also built to make diversions and check gully erosion. In Rampur, stone is the principal construction material for buildings, trails, walls, etc., where bricks are not available. About 80 per cent of the roofs of houses in the village are made of stone slabs. Diversions, canal walls and terrace repair works are usually made with stone and brushwood whereas mud and stone is used in house walls, and stone slabs (slates) are fixed to underlying wooden slabs in roof making.

To make the best use of all wasteland, grass and trees are planted. Depending upon their suitability, grasses (such as *amriso*, citronella, napier or *babio*) are planted. Bamboo is grown everywhere on slopes and in gullies. *Badar*, a big fodder tree, is grown on both sides of main trails like a greenbelt of a highway. Two religious trees – *bar* and *peepal* – are planted a certain distance from the main trails. Usually, *chautari* – places for rest – and ponds are built beside these trees.

All these activities have helped to keep the village green and to check excessive erosion in the monsoon. The common-sense technique used in all construction and resource management work in the village is to let the flood out without much damage. For example, in *khet* lands there are enough outlets to pass water to the next bench terrace.

The cloudburst of 6 July 1993

On 6 July 1993 unusually torrential rainfall hit the village. Since the evening light rain had fallen continuously. Around midnight a heavy downpour of rain and a thunderstorm woke the villagers up. According to the villagers, the unprecedented rainfall, lasting for about two hours, prevented them from seeing beyond a metre or hearing anything other than the rainfall itself.

Early in the morning, they found a sea of debris deposited, along with huge boulders, on about half of the village. Houses, sheds and trees were

Table 4. Loss of life and property in Okhaldhunga caused by the debris flow of 6 July 1993

Name of Village	Number of deaths	Number seriously injured	Number of livestock lost	Number of houses damaged	Estimated loss (in rupees)
Rampur *tar*	18	9	72	*	*
Lamidanda	8	5	5	*	*
Harkapur	3	1	21	*	*
Katunje	1	–	6	*	*
Total	30	16	104	536	130 000 000

* Details of each place not available separately
Source: DPTC 1994.

either buried or swept away. Dead or severely injured people and livestock were lying around. The way out of the less affected area of the village was cut off. The surrounding hill slopes were severely scraped by the large extent of the landslides and debris flow. The slope to the north of the village was heavily affected by innumerable landslides at different points, while the downstream and plains areas were flooded with debris flows and boulders. A number of huge boulders and trees of large diameter disappeared. There were other boulders hanging on the upstream slope of the mountain from where the landslides had started that night.

People were shocked and awkward. Everyone was puzzled. In fact, the landscape and topography of the village had changed significantly due to the cloudburst. Rampur *tar* was changed overnight into a place of horror. It had been considered to be a rather safe region in the mid hills. Dozens of landslides came down along the slope. However, only two of them affected the settlement and these were smaller than those that flooded the forest and agricultural lands. Of these two, the smaller one that entered the dense settlement area killed 16 people, while the other killed two people.

Long-term effects

The debris flow of 6 July 1993 seriously affected the central and eastern part of the village.[8] Other parts of the village, including the dense

---

8 While discussing on the disaster-prone part of the village, it is important to note that the severe earthquake of the year 1989 in eastern and central Nepal affected most of the houses on the western side of the village, while the effect on those of the central and eastern parts was minor.

settlement area of the west belt, were also affected by the flood of water, but there were no serious losses except crops. About 50 per cent of the agricultural land went under the debris deposit. The maize crop which was ready for harvesting was also lost.

The disaster had serious effects. Reactivation of the once stabilized landslides, loss of nutrients and organic matter from the washing away of the topsoil, and the drying up of the springs and wells (sources of drinking water) into a dry and waste land have been the major environmental effects. Each of these has had further impact, both on the environment and human beings.

The mass of soil, debris and boulders reached the Molung River. In 1994, the river also swept away thousands of hectares of *khet* along its banks in the valley: the earlier deposits in the river contributed to the rising water levels and to the river consequently changing its course. Farmers say the riverbed has risen by several metres. During the 1994 monsoon, the slopes already destabilized in 1993 fell at certain points although there were no major landslides and floods in the village that year.

The loss of fertile land as a result of the events in 1993 and 1994 also created hardship for villagers. Loss of fertile topsoil in both years was another major impact. Villagers complain of loss of production, although the extent of this has not been scientifically validated. To compensate, farmers are turning to chemical fertilizers whose use is on the rise.

The mountain slope to the north of Rampur is moisture rich, generating springs and small streams from different points along its base which are the only sources of drinking water outside the monsoon months. The 1993 landslide disrupted a number of these and as a result the sources of drinking water have declined – both in terms of the number of sources and the quantity of water provided – with, consequently, a great shortage in the dry months. All available water sources are tapped for drinking water.

Similarly, the shortage of fuel wood is also high. The villagers rely on the slopes to the north and downstream at the south and west of the village for both fuel and building wood. These forests were already under pressure, and thinning out, when the cloudburst occurred, and the landslide caused significant damage. In addition, a number of trees were cut down for timber for rebuilding houses after the disaster. The forest users' committee had to reduce the quota of fuel wood supplies, leading to shortage. The poorest have suffered the most.

The overall living standard in the village has fallen. The value of land has declined. Many of those who lost lands to the debris deposit have no productive land in other areas. This means that for subsistence they have to seek some other source of living. Some families lost breadwinners. An increasing number of families survive on daily wages as the land cannot sustain them. Drop-out rates among school children, particularly girls, sharply increased in 1993 and 1994. Fifteen families have migrated and, according to the villagers, a further 15 families migrated from Harkapur, the neighbouring village, in 1995 after their farmlands were washed away by the flood of the Molung River in 1994.

Response

Soon after a disaster both mountains and their people attempt to manage. Every year, the rivers damage farmlands along their banks but the affected communities repair the damage. Small and moderate landslides are usually stabilized by local efforts. Natural regeneration of the vegetation is also common. Villagers do not look for outside help in minor difficulties. As long as they are able to face the odds, they do so. However, when people face one disaster after the other their skill, resources and poverty do not allow them to recover immediately. External help is then necessary.

Villagers usually regard disaster as a regular feature of 'supreme nature'. There is a popular saying: *Daibako khel lai sabaile mannai pardo rahechha* ('there is no way out other than to obey the powerful god's acts'). However, after the disaster, the villagers promptly started rescue and rehabilitation activities. At the same time they attempted to identify the possibility of further landslides. People were further threatened by the continuous rainfall, with the possibility of more slope failures. Several large boulders were hanging on the steep slope above the dense settlement. The fall of any of these boulders would mean not only damage to dozens of houses and farm lands but could also start to bring down the upper slope on which the boulders stood.

The major activities in the immediate response to the disasters were as follows.

Bereaved family members or their kin, according to their culture, performed the 13-day-long death rites, living in temporary sheds. Some of those who survived with injuries also performed the death rites from hospital beds. Villagers assisted them in various ways to complete the mourning period.

People's next major concern after attending to the victims and the dead was the loss of the maize crop which they were harvesting, and delays in cultivating paddy, millet and other cereals. July is the peak cropping season when harvesting maize, terrace reformation and maintenance, and rice planting work is performed. There is a proverb in the village: 'Stay at home in the month of *Ashad* (June/July) and face starvation'. It was feared that more people would die the next year due to starvation if they failed to cultivate their lands at this time. From the third day the majority of the villagers divided their time between rehabilitating canals and farmlands, and managing the chaos in their homes.

The unity of villagers during the rescue and relief work was exemplary. Their social, cultural and political differences, which were significant, did not reappear for a long time after the disaster. The backward (untouchable) community was greatly assisted by others in terms of materials, providing shelter and rehabilitating their lands.

At the local level, a committee under the chairmanship of the Chief District Officer (CDO) was formed. The CDO is the person authorized to undertake emergency relief operations in the district and co-ordinate with the central government as well as other agencies working in the disaster area. Following the information received from the villagers a team of police and representatives of government line agencies in the district was sent to the affected area on 7 July. The central government hospital and non-governmental organizations (NGOs) working in the district were informed.

From the second day, about 50 police and army men joined with villagers in digging out dead bodies, searching for lost people and rescuing trapped and injured people. The district administration distributed 3000 rupees and 40 kilograms of rice to each family that had suffered a death. Plastic tents and a set of cooking pots were distributed to the homeless families. The District Red Cross Office, United Mission Hospital of Okhaldhunga and Nepal Food Corporation Office played an active role in providing relief to the affected families.

Villagers' perspective of natural disaster

The people of Rampur worship many gods and goddesses and there is a special god for each caste (and sometimes for families within castes), mainly to avoid ill fate and evil spirits that often appear in the form of disasters.

Table 5. Organizations involved in assisting the affected families

Name of Organization	Status	Type of assistance/activity
District Administration	Government	Coordinated and supervized the relief work, mobilized police and army.
Red Cross Society	District Office	Distributed clothes, utensils and provided primary treatment.
United Mission to Nepal	International NGO	Distributed clothes, food, medicine and water purifying tablets; provided emergency treatment; supported villagers financially in dumping the dead bodies of livestock; rehabilitated the drinking water system.
District Development Committee	Local elected body	Assisted to rehabilitate canals and tracks around the village.
District Drinking Water Office	Government	Acquired information and promised assistance.
District Irrigation Office	Government	Acquired information and promised assistance for canal rehabilitation work.
District Watershed Conservation Office	Government	Acquired information and located landslide-prone areas and safe areas.
Nepal Food Corporation	Government	Distributed food as per government quota.
Nepal Police and Army	Government	Rescue work; injured persons taken to hospital by helicopter.

They mention three categories of natural disaster: landslides/floods, earthquake and famine (the last often caused by drought and crop diseases). For most of the inhabitants of Rampur, a flood-induced disaster usually means the loss of their *khet* in the deep river valley due to the changing course of the river. Similarly, by the word 'landslide', they remember the slope fall or debris flow from the mountain to the north or from the steep slope around the edge of Rampur *tar* that rises from the river bed about 500 metres below. Small- to medium-scale landslides and landslips are not seen as a 'loss' as long as they do not damage a settlement area or block the river, forcing it to change its usual course.

Each year hundreds of scars of landslides appear on the surrounding hill slopes in the rainy season. Most of them disappear in one or two months under vegetation cover. The process is a normal phenomenon. Villagers partly believe the suggestion that a landslide can be controlled by vegetation or forest cover, but their experiences have taught them that landslides cannot be controlled by the forest alone. There are many examples of landslides in the forest area where numbers of trees were uprooted and swept away. This was the case in the landslide of 1993 when major landslides in the forest areas destroyed hundreds of trees, including big *bar* and *peepal* trees. However, for agricultural and economic reasons villagers grow bamboo and fodder trees where they find bare land, both on public land and at the edge of their private lands. They are usually grown on the steep slopes at the edge of farming terraces and in gullies where the chances of landslides are high; they are also grown on marginal and waste lands.

Different opinions are expressed by the villagers regarding the cause of the disaster of July 1993. They are outlined here under four main headings.

Blasting

The landslide would not have been so damaging if excessive blasting had not been used during the construction of the canal for the Rampur *tar* irrigation project. The blasting reactivated the old landslide-prone area and each year a huge chunk of land-mass falls into the Pokting River.

The pine forest

According to villagers, the District Forest Office encouraged them to grow pine trees on the deforested area in the past. They soon realized that pine forest cannot control landslide and erosion; instead it has the reverse effect.[9] If there had been forests of other tree species, the size of the landslide and its effect would not have been of such a scale.

---

9 The roots of pines hold substantial amounts of water and dry out the soil round about. If the land topography is steep, land adjacent to the tree becomes liable to slide down. The pine leaves (needles) that fall are also acidic, which prevents the growth of other plants nearby.

Disrespect to Kuldevata

Some elders of the village blamed the calamity on disregard of a local god by some people who had stayed away from the religious festival of *Kul Pooja* when it is the social responsibility of each member of all the *Dahal* families to attend the festival. Although different castes and families have their own *kuldevata* (*kul* means family; *devata* means god), people of different communities gather to worship others' gods on special occasions.

Rainfall cycle

There are also some *pandits* or village intellectuals who suggest that such disasters are inevitable over the course of time. Not only floods/landslides, but earthquakes, drought and epidemics are sure to occur eventually. They are parts of the natural evolution process. The rain of that night was also a part of the process. They compare the present disaster with the major floods/landslides that occurred in 1856 and 1932.

Effectiveness of outside help

Within two weeks of the incident there were no agencies working in Rampur any more. Some people from Okhaldhunga attempted to pressure the government in Kathmandu for additional support to the flood-affected areas. They also collected donations in the form of cash and materials from the general public.

The rescue work lasted for a week. Agencies repeatedly assured the people that affected families would be provided with enough support, including assistance for rehabilitation of farmlands and implementation of a watershed management programme for stabilizing the hill slope. Assurances were given that loose, unstable and overhanging large boulders would be removed from the slope. The assurances remain unfulfilled.

According to the villagers, the United Mission to Nepal (UMN), which runs a 20–bed hospital and implements a community development programme in Okhaldhunga District, played the most effective role during and after the emergency relief work. When government agencies returned after a couple of days, villagers were mainly supported by UMN as well as other social organizations. Additional beds were arranged in the hospital for the flood victims. A UMN mobile team of health workers also served on the spot at different villages, including Rampur.

A team from UMN provided food, clothes and medicines. It helped to relocate displaced pipes and supplied water purifying chemicals for the public water tank and individual households. It also provided financial support to dump hundreds of dead bodies of livestock which was labour consuming and expensive work. UMN then assisted in rehabilitating the heavily dislocated drinking water system (which had been built by UMN itself 10 years ago).

Local capacity

Various inferences can be drawn from the case of Rampur village.

Following the event of July 1993, Rampur has been regaining its value and past glory. Since then, villagers have been working tirelessly for the revival of their original village. The debris-covered land has been rehabilitated as agricultural land. The fragile hill slope to the north has been developed into grassland and bushy forest. There are a number of check dams and erosion control measures. Livestock farming techniques have also been changed. The traditional way of feeding livestock was to free them in the jungle for the whole day. Now, they are kept and fed at home. Rows of fodder trees are grown around homes, farmlands and public land.

Economic and social contexts have also been changed over time. Farming is changing from a traditional non-cash economy to a market-oriented cash economy. These changes have mixed effects on the living standards of the villagers. Families having a good labour force are among the beneficiaries. The living standard of some socially and economically backward families has also been improved.

The condition of 'middle class' families has declined. The term 'middle class' is used here to refer to villagers of average income, mainly of the *Brahmin* and *Chhetri* castes, who have just enough land to supply food for their families and do not need to work for others (labouring for others is not thought to be respectable work; people from higher castes with sufficient wealth avoid this for traditional reasons; and ploughing is traditionally a job for the lower castes). Their condition has declined for several reasons: loss of farmland to landslide and flood, loss of grassland for livestock, declining forest resources, lack of physically able labour within the family, the rising cost of hiring labour,[10] having no sources of cash income, or being unable to adapt to the transformation of economic activities from a subsistence base to greater market orientation. If a crop is lost or damaged, these farmers have to seek loans to pay labourers, obtain food for their own families and purchase fertilizers for the next growing season. Crop failure in two consecutive years can mean loss of livelihood for many.

Changing coping strategy

Floods and landslides are not the only disasters facing Rampur. There are other types of disaster that have been affecting the village for decades. Drought or shortage of water is the most frequent problem, which in some cases becomes severe. River 'cutting' (changing course and taking away the land nearby) leads to loss of farmlands, which is a frequent problem. Earthquakes, epidemics, crop diseases and forest fires are other disastrous events. The villagers cope with each of these events differently. They change their strategy over time. The strategy is political, economic and environmental in nature.

Conclusion

Extreme rainfall events in the mountains of Nepal usually end with several deaths and heavy loss of property, severe damage to the local environment and deformation of the existing landscape. The mountains of Nepal experience torrential rainfall every monsoon, accounting for 80 per cent of the total annual rainfall. Soon after the monsoon rain influences the entire hilly region, the region becomes saturated and sensitive. Extreme climatic events such as cloudbursts can trigger big landslides, floods and mass movement in these conditions.

Facing risks and coping with disasters are part of life for mountain dwellers in Nepal. The early response of the villagers to the disaster is emotional and gradually they gather strength to re-manage the situation with the means at their hands. Later, when they manage the situation, their experiences become an additional strength to face the next risk. However, the case is not always the same for all people in society. People having some sort of economic, social or physical strength can cope with

---

10 General demand for labourers is increasing rapidly, especially for construction and load-carrying work.

the situation and regain their lost property. The fate of those less capable is uncertain. They often lose the place, the economic status or position (including property), that they hold.

Following the disaster, the affected communities receive token help from outside. It is not much more than a condolence message. They are in need of others' help for some time after to re-manage and organize the basic necessities for subsistence.

The current perspective of looking at vulnerability has failed to focus on these people. They love and value their land resources. They suffer when lives are lost but they may lose their hopes of survival if farmlands are lost. They should be supported to reclaim the farmlands, restore productivity and build their houses in a safe way. Supporting the affected community also means support to the larger community in several ways. In the mountain region, shortage of agricultural labourers in the cropping season is acute. In this context, seeking volunteer labour in rehabilitation works (which is often labour consuming) is not pragmatic. The usual way, of asking local people to volunteer their labour in the name of 'people's participation' for all construction work in the village is not beneficial to the villagers. Rather it exploits them. Providing financial and technical support, including alternative ways of coping with the crisis situation, can be an effective way to help the affected community. However, the assistance will not be helpful if the approach is not socially sensitive.

5. Can Vulnerability be Understood?[1]

MIHIR R BHATT

OVER A NUMBER of years I have worked with disaster victims, as a planner who has helped them and the non-governmental organizations (NGOs) who work with them in mitigation, recovery, rehabilitation, preparedness and prevention. When planning disaster mitigation activities within the Disaster Mitigation Institute (DMI) and with victim or vulnerable communities, I found that most of the data that came in for use were not from the victims but from those who worked with them, for them, sometimes on them. Although the intentions of these workers[2] were mostly noble and sensible, they differed from the views, ideas and approaches of the victims. The workers did ask the victims, but it was not enough, particularly for DMI, which sees itself as a 'people's institute' making different people's knowledge and practices more widely known.

I decided to develop a method that might change things. Instead of our asking the victims what was the nature and extent of their loss, we should let the victims say it on their own, in their own way, and in their own voice. This was one change. Another similar change was that instead of focusing on the disaster, the event, the point in time, we decided to explore the life story of the victim. The victims set the 'event' in their life cycle. This changed the picture and made it more complex. Now there was not only the immediate event, say a drought, to deal with, but also the long-term and continued condition of vulnerability. Moreover, the victim was now seen and known as a worker, mother,

---

1 I have benefited greatly from the ideas, thoughts, perspectives, writings and insights of Rupa K. Jani (McMaster University, Canada), Ann C. Carver's 'double vision' theory and writings, Gayatri Chakravorty Spivak's ideas on cultural politics, Robin Skynner and John Cleese's book *Families and How to Survive Them*, Nevelle Symington's writings on psychoanalytical process, and the *Nirvanashtakam* of Hindu scriptures.

2 By 'worker' we mean here relief worker, including workers involved in the entire disaster response cycle.

water user, consumer, voter, brother and so on. We thought that this gave us a better understanding of the victims and their needs.

Over a period of time, the method became standard: hear of a disaster (mostly minor or medium) and rush to the site, contact the victims, and while doing relief work let them tell or write their life stories.[3] Writing on their own, or with our help, they say what they want to say, in the way that they choose. The life stories were from the victims of floods, droughts, riots, famine, fire and plague. What we studied was a different disaster context in which all these victims' life stories were created.

A new wealth of information and insights came out. Mostly, these pointed to the fact that the tendency to generalize about vulnerability theories was of limited use, and that we obtained a far better view of the differentiated impact of, and response to, disasters by listening to victims and reading their writings.

When we returned from the site of a disaster and the flutter of relief, we used the life stories to educate ourselves, and sometimes others who had an interest in disaster mitigation, from the point of view of the victims. We, as workers, tried to seek out material to interpret life stories that originated in a situation vastly different from ours, and that neither first-hand experience nor educational background had prepared us to understand.

Through this experience, I learned more about the rewards and the problems of working with life stories by victims whose 'cultures' *as victims* are so very different from those of outsiders. Breaking through our (outsiders') cultural perspectives in reading works by victim writers (we call them now 'works', and 'writers'!) has long been recognized as a difficult – some would say impossible – challenge.[4] I have found that simply reading and discussing such victims' material rarely modifies the relief worker's ways of seeing, which tend to assess others – the victims – in terms of the worker's own outlooks, experiences and anticipations of action. Some workers unfailingly read the need for better preparedness while others find the hidden hand of a male-centred society. One of our team members invariably finds useful slogans in such works. Such views depend on how the workers see themselves – for example, whether it is

---

3 See the box 'The life story method' on pp. 70–71 for details.

4 A challenge made greater because of the difficulty project workers face in finding time to read these works carefully within crowded schedules and limited project budgets.

The life story method

The method developed by DMI works typically as follows (although in practice it is applied on a case-by-case basis with appropriate modifications). DMI hears of a disaster (mostly small or medium in size and impact, affecting eight to 10 villages or three to four organizations), and rushes to the site, carrying out relief work directly or with or through other organizations. DMI may also be involved in initial mitigation planning. During such an activity on the site, the victims are encouraged to narrate an incident or event from their life: this leads to writing about the disaster and setting it in their own life story. Some victims may write on their own, some may need help in actual writing (not being literate) and others may need encouragement or assistance to continue writing.

The exercises are generally three-day events with a group of not more than 20 people invited. Introduction of a new idea and new activity both call for this amount of time; this is also needed to build bonds and trust between the participants and to develop the creative process. Before such sessions, the DMI team and others with a suitable background in community work prepare how they will evoke ideas and draw out the participants' experiences. When the members of the group are not familiar with each other, a meeting is organized between facilitators and participants.

On Day 1 the participants are introduced to each other and the activity of writing is introduced with displays of actual pieces of writing, and a video showing a similar writing session or a victim of a disaster who has recently been involved in a session. This takes about half a day. For the rest of the day the writing of life stories begins in small groups or individually. Depending on the participants and group dynamics, the groups are formed by self-selection, randomly or more purposeful grouping. Each group has one or more facilitators.

On Day 2 the groups go over what was written and how it was written, and reflect on their achievements and difficulties. Some volunteered pieces of writing are discussed by the whole group to illustrate the possible outcomes and give encouragement.

On Day 3 the previous day's work is again reviewed, mainly focusing on the disaster event set in the life story but also pinpointing what has been left out of the writing (by design or default). This leads, by agreement, to deciding how to complete the writing. The

70

process of writing is also discussed in terms of organizing experience and thoughts.

Encouraging the victims to write such life stories has become a systematic and specialized activity. It also calls for some judgement on the part of the organizer of the activity: judgement in balancing the demands of a written language and expression with the freedom the victims need to say what they want about the disaster or its place in their life cycle, in their own way and with their own voice.

Over the past five years, DMI has organized over 20 writing sessions with some 500 victim-participants from eight districts in Gujarat and the city of Ahmedabad. The groups include people affected by flood, drought, plague, malaria and riots. Such sessions have been held as part of projects funded by the World Bank, the United States Agency for International Development and the International Labour Organization; and the method has been passed on to other projects and organizations.

as a professional in the service of the poor, a charity giver, an elder brother, a link between the state and the citizens, and so on.

A typical response to such victim-material is along the lines of 'how interesting and/or strange, pitiful, moving, quaint, they are . . . and therefore inferior, vulnerable, less capable, because they are not like me' – a response that reinforces separation and implies a hierarchical valuing of victims and their societies, and which is often accompanied by a desire to 'help' or 'support' them, or in some cases 'facilitate' for them, which in reality means: 'Make them more like me (less vulnerable and more capable)'.

Another typical, but very different response is: 'We are all people with certain characteristics in common; therefore, we are all alike, and superficial differences are of little importance.' This approach denies the real difference between the 'cultures' of victims and non-victims, and in doing so, fails to respect the unique human being, a victim in her or his vulnerable setting, the individual victim who is not 'like me'.

In both cases, the reader, the relief worker, is filtering what she or he reads through the conceptual framework, assumptions, and values of her or his culture and, as a result, is creating false 'stories' that fit her or his own expectations. How many times during the writing sessions, when a facilitator is citing something from a victim's life story to show a particular point, the victim has said, 'That is not what I meant, that is not what I meant at all.' For example, if a victim describes her husband collecting relief handouts of rice, it may be seen by the worker as male dominance and not as a sign of a helpful husband.

The style of writing itself also presents difficulties. Repetition of ideas, we workers think, is poor composition, whereas to the writer it is emphasizing a point or fact.

The routine ease of creating false 'stories' that fit the worker's own expectations has consequences. The worker gains limited understanding of the real victim or their culture. Inadvertently, the worker perpetuates a lie, more a distorted myth of reality, that validates the worker's own culture as the norm and defines all others as deviations. By recognizing the problems of monocultural vision, however, the worker may acquire cross-cultural awareness.

Three problems stand between the worker and such an awareness. These are:

o the illusion of homogeneity or sameness
o we/they thinking
o the need to explain.

The illusion of homogeneity is generated to some degree in many cultures. It is particularly characteristic of relief workers whose educational systems have traditionally advocated belief in an inherently superior, homogeneous, culture of the 'capable'. Workers like us often fail to recognize that within us, the 'capables', there are many cultures: religion, sexual preference, age, gender, lifestyle, and so on. In fact, the standard response of the dominant culture of the non-victims, the workers, to victim-cultures has been to melt them forcibly into one; characteristics that do not fit are devalued, pushed to the margins, or denied. The belief in one superior, 'capable' culture, with its prescribed characteristics, has been exported and imposed upon victim societies and victims everywhere. The resulting illusion of homogeneity in its 'capable' or 'less vulnerable' manifestation has influenced us around the world.

This illusion of homogeneity and its denial of difference blinds relief workers to the reality of multiplicity as the norm. There is no homogeneous 'we' to contrast to a homogeneous 'they'. But the illusion creates the we/they mode of thinking, with its assumed cultural superiority or inferiority. One of its distorting by-products is that even where the worker does see himself or herself and members of his or her culture as complex, active, subjects, the victims are still perceived as indistinguishable from one another, as controllable, homogeneous objects of study who can be reduced to generalized data and explained. If something can be explained, it has been reduced and owned: I know it, it is mine.

Certainly, such an explanation is an illusion. It is a way of scanning a diverse group of victims, distorting or even ignoring their variety and their vulnerability, and recognizing only their similarities. The victims are thus reduced to consistent traits that fit an encompassing explanation. This 'production of theoretical explanation' is so basic to non-victim thought and scholarship that the relief workers brought up on its tenets think that everything, even anything new or different, can be explained, articulated and understood.[5]

Can the relief or rehabilitation or disaster mitigation workers (who are not victims) accept the premiss that victims different from themselves can never be known, understood, or explained fully or completely – and can they recognize that there is actually nothing wrong with their inevitable inability to acquire such understanding? Is it possible to grant to victims the status of subject in our thinking and study? Can we identify the ways each of us non-victims deals with difference? If we non-victims can become aware of the ways our cultures influence our dealing with difference, this can provide a foundation for perceiving the reality of the vulnerability of victims and their experiences in both disaster and non-disaster situations.

If the non-victims can learn to see and accept the reality of the vulnerability of the victims and their experiences, and stop there, without understanding or explaining them, this will be a great leap forward. By seeing and accepting, one acknowledges a reality distinct in itself, and in so doing one may gain a basis for representing that reality and the victims who reside within it. Non-victims may also have gained a clearer basis for recognizing similarities across the experience of victims, should they exist.

In their professional disaster work, some non-victims do try to place themselves in the subject's position in order to make sense of the vulnerability experience. But it is a more difficult and different process altogether to place those who are vulnerable or victims or both in that central position as subject: in other words, where the starting point as well as the direction are set by the victim and not the non-victim. When

---

5 Just recently, a pioneering relief agency rejected a DMI proposal for the study of local coping mechanisms against drought by stating that 'we know enough about it already', even though their 'knowing' was based on lessons learned mostly from Africa and not from South Asia.

a non-victim or a relief worker reads a life story of an unfamiliar experience of vulnerability, only a very conscious act of will that thrusts the character and the story into the centre of reality – without imposing cultural norms from non-victims' experience – will allow the process of understanding vulnerability cross-culturally to begin.

Even so, this process is complex and difficult to achieve, for it involves what I have learned to call a 'triple vision'. A non-victim or a non-vulnerable person can never step out of, or leave behind fully, their own self and its seeing and interpreting activity, which is a function of being a person, the subject of one's own singular vision. For a non-victim to leave the self behind entirely, he or she would have to have become possessed by another entity or character, that of the victim. Hence, the non-victim must be conscious of the process by which experience of vulnerability is filtered through his or her own perceptions, and, at the same time, attempt to deliberately make someone else – the victim in unfamiliar vulnerability – the centre of reality, recognizing his or her own singular vision. If a non-victim achieves this, he or she may experience vulnerability as an impression of seeing through three sets of eyes at once: of simultaneously looking, being looked at and being the difference between the two. She or he will move between being subject and object, will learn what it is to be both insider and outsider, or neither, or in-between.

To illustrate how a life profile reads and may be read using this 'triple vision' I have included an example: 'From water to water' (see box on pages 75–7). Reading from the perspective of a non-victim, a subject, we can see systems and conditions as the cause of the woman's pain and vulnerability.

When reading this account many non-victims will find it difficult, if not impossible, to keep the woman in the subject's position even though it is a first-person account, and to stay unwaveringly within that woman's point of view. The non-victim's own cultural values will produce objections, insights, questions, value judgements, irritations and recommendations: these pull the non-victim away from the woman's perspective, even if only momentarily. Thus the challenge becomes one of holding three perspectives in focus simultaneously or of shifting back and forth between them while recognizing all. In this way, the non-victim can explore the limited nature of his or her understanding of the victim's vulnerability. The victim and the non-victim both function as subjects, mutually acting upon each other, interacting, rather than either one being relegated to the position of passive object.

The responses generated by this approach to understanding vulnerability include many 'how?' and 'why?' questions. For example, in the case-study below one might ask why the woman mentions the dust on her clothes and hair as well as her memory, or how she perceives the value of the new roads to the village that stop flood water from escaping. Such questions can also be valuable signposts to that which non-victims recognize but do not understand. These questions remind the non-victims that they need a larger cultural context to develop a fuller interpretation of any story of vulnerability from outside their own culture. Also, to understand the life stories better some knowledge of the traditional family and images of woman as victim is essential.

Once the non-victims have seen the wall of differences between themselves and the victims, they can at least begin to understand how it separates the two. So, paradoxically, in order to see, link and understand each other, we have to see that which does not allow us to see, that separates, and remains un-understood: the wall. Only by recognizing the wall can we see through it – at times, in parts, at an angle – though never fully. Accepting the reality of this experience of limitation makes possible the non-victim's – our – acceptance of the reality of the life profile experience and the woman who wrote it and what she presents. And through that acceptance of separation and limited understanding, we learn to respect the woman, her culture and her vulnerability. We may not have understood her vulnerability and even less reduced it, but by refusing to rewrite or understand them in the mould of our own culture's assumptions of vulnerability, we have avoided discounting their reality. Perhaps we shall also have come closer to recognizing real connections among victims of heterogeneous identities and a shared destiny on this vulnerable sub-continent.

From water to water

Dark dust was on my clothes when I remember my first days at school in my small village near the desert border in Banaskantha. Since, my memory is dusted. How can I write? No, I never learned to write. Yes I will note my points. Yes, note my illegitimacy; poverty of generations; a mother who advanced from lowly farm labourer to a bonded labourer; my marriage to and divorce from an older man with a farm as large as his bath towel; my daughter from him, a first but a girl child, later ceremoniously neglected and soon dead.

Divorced, with a daughter as a first born, hair more dusty, I go, wanting to work, mostly fetching water for the big farmers during drought. I rise from headloader to water manager on the field having known the correct timing and amount of watering the cash crop of *jeera* [cumin] needs. I call myself, now, a manager. They did, and still do, think I was just a headloader.

These women came from the big city, without *bindi* on their forehead[6] and with shoes on their feet. I go to their meetings, small and late at night, talking about work and wages. Wages interest me, exciting. But how could I speak up? They were launching a nursery and wanted a woman to manage it. I could do that. It meant late hour visits to guard the field and long hours of watering. I enlist my name. They teach me how to plant trees, the *sarkari baboos*[7] with clean hands and unbent bottoms: busy forestry expert and village, class bores.[8] As droughts continue, my work continues. I rise to *agewan* [leader] position. I enroll more members. My mother can now talk to me. My in-laws now call me. I pour water on plants, each season, each year. Then on to the heights: elected as *agewan*, a new marriage of sorts, and my own house, small very small. I collect gold dusts from droughts[9] watering nursery plants.

And now this year floods in our deserts. New roads do not allow the water to flow its own course. The water is trapped. The village road was cut off. The tar melted in standing water. Was it tar? Yes it melted. My nursery is in water. Water, water. Water. I was elected to be in charge of relief. I go to villages, from water to more water. Now everyone turns up in my story: from water to water. And I have malaria.

Note. The above life profile was written by a victim of the June 1997 floods in the deserts of Banaskantha. 'Five feet five and slender, black hair, sky

---

6 A *bindi* is the red paste mark that a Hindu woman traditionally wears on her forehead to indicate that she is married. In more liberal circles, such as cities or the middle classes, many married women have dropped this custom.

7 Term for government administrators who are too full of themselves to do any good.

8 i.e. great bores.

9 This remark could have several meanings: the most direct one is that the saplings are as valuable as gold dust at a time of crisis; but note the perhaps ironic use of the word 'dust' here, which elsewhere in the narrative has negative connotations, and there is something ironic, too, in earning money by raising saplings in a drought year.

light [sky blue] eyes, with angled features, she suggests she is easily broken. She is not breakable. She digs a brass[10] of earth a day, carries 30 pots on her head a day, cuts half a field of harvest in a day, and outlives most of her detractors at night guarding the nursery, occasionally dropping a bit of poison'[11] is how her team-mate profiled her in another writing session.

---

10 A measurement of earth dug: 100 cubic feet.

11 i.e. her ironic views can turn bitter or poisonous, hurting others on occasion.

References

Chapter 1. Understanding Vulnerability

Bastian S., Bastian N., ed. (1996), *Assessing Participation: a debate from South Asia.* New Delhi: Konark.

Bhatt M.R. (1996), 'On Understanding Vulnerability'. Presentation to Duryog Nivaran Steering Committee Meeting, Colombo, November 1996.

Bhatt M.R. (1997a), 'Vulnerability: renewed focus'. Introductory address to Duryog Nivaran workshop 'Understanding Vulnerability: a South Asian perspective', Colombo, August 1997.

Bhatt M.R., ed. (1997b), *Proceedings of Workshop on Understanding Vulnerability: a South Asian perspective, 21–22 August 1997.* Colombo: Duryog Nivaran.

Blaikie P., Cannon T, Davis I, Wisner B (1994), *At Risk: natural hazards, people's vulnerability and disasters.* London: Routledge.

Chambers R. (1983), *Rural Development: putting the last first.* Harlow: Longman.

The Concise Oxford Dictionary (1976). Oxford: Oxford University Press.

Duryog Nivaran (1996), *Disasters and Vulnerability in South Asia. Programme of work for Duryog Nivaran: a South Asian initiative on disaster mitigation.* Colombo: Duryog Nivaran.

(IDNDR) International Decade for Natural Disaster Reduction (1994), *Yokohama Strategy and Plan of Action for a Safer World.* Geneva: IDNDR.

(IFRC) International Federation of Red Cross and Red Crescent Societies (1997), *World Disasters Report 1997.* Oxford: Oxford University Press.

Mitchell J. (1997), 'The Listening Legacy: challenges for participatory approaches' in Scobie J. (ed.), *Mitigating the Millennium.* Rugby: Intermediate Technology Development Group.

(OECD-DAC) Organisation for Economic Co-operation and Development, Development Assistance Committee (1994), *Guidelines for Aid Agencies on Disaster Mitigation.* Paris: OECD.

Patel A.K. (1997), 'Understanding Vulnerability: recent tools and methods'. Paper presented to Duryog Nivaran workshop 'Understanding Vulnerability: a South Asian perspective', Colombo, August 1997.

Roget P.M., ed. Dutch R.A. (1966), *Roget's Thesaurus.* Harmondsworth: Penguin Books.

Warmington, V. (1995), *Disaster Reduction: a review of disaster prevention, mitigation and preparedness*. Ottowa: Reconstruction and Rehabilitation Fund of the Canadian Council for International Cooperation.

Wijkman A., Timberlake L. (1984), *Natural Disasters: acts of God or acts of man?* London: Earthscan.

Chapter 3. Drought and Household Coping Strategies

Central Bank of Sri Lanka (1996), *Annual Report.* Colombo.

Department of Census and Statistics (1988), *Statistical Pocket Book of the Democratic Socialist Republic of Sri Lanka.* Colombo: Department of Government Printing.

Gunawardena R.L.H. (1971), 'Irrigation and Hydraulic Society in Early Medieval Ceylon', *Past and Present* 53.

Hemakumara N.U., Fernando N., Ariyaratne B.R. (n.d.), *Seasonal Summary Report on Integrated Water Management in Huruluwewa Watershed (Maha 1994/95 Season).* Colombo: SCOR/International Irrigation Management Institute.

Irrigation Department (1975), *Register of Irrigation Projects in Sri Lanka.* Colombo: Irrigation Department.

Leach E.R. (1959), 'Hydraulic Society of Ceylon', *Past and Present* 15.

Madduma Bandara C.M. (1982), 'Effect of Drought on the Livelihood of Peasant Families in the Dry Zone of Sri Lanka: A Study of the Mahapotana Korale in the North Central Province' in M.M. Yoshino, I. Kayane and C.M. Madduma Bandara (ed.), *Tropical Environments.* University of Peradeniya.

Madduma Bandara C.M. (1985), 'Catchment Ecosystems and Village Tank Cascades in the Dry Zone of Sri Lanka' in J. Lundqvist, U. Lohm, F. Falkenmark (ed.), *Strategies for River Basin Development.* Germany: Reidel Publishing Company.

Siriweera I. (1971), 'The Decay of the Dry Zone Reservoir System of Ancient Ceylon' in K. Indrapala (ed.), *The Collapse of the Rajarata Civilization in Ceylon and the Drift to the South-West: A symposium.* Ceylon Studies Seminar, Peradeniya.

Tennakoon M.U.A. (1986a), *Drought Hazard and Rural Development.* Colombo: Central Bank of Sri Lanka.

Tennakoon M.U.A. (1986b) *Settlers' Perception of and Adjustment to Drought Hazard in the Mahaweli Development Area.* Symposium on Mahaweli 6–9 November 1986. Colombo: Sri Lanka Association for the Advancement of Science (SLAAS).

Wijayaratne C.M. (1996), 'An Evaluation System for Sustainable Watershed Management'. Paper presented at the International Seminar on 'Tools for Analysis and Evaluation of Sustainable Land Use in Rural Development' 2–14 December 1996, Zschortau, Federal Republic of Germany.

Witfogel K.A. (1957), *Oriental despotism: A comparative study of total power.* New Haven: Yale University Press.

Chapter 4. Coping with Climatic Disasters

Deshantar (1993), 'Okhaldhunga: Yewata Gawn Yeshari Ukkelio', *Deshantar Weekly*, 25 July, 1993: Kathmandu.

Dikshit A.M. (1990), 'Landslide Hazards in Nepal: Causes and Assessment', *Water Nepal* Vol. 2 No. 1: Kathmandu.

DPTC (1993), *Annual Disaster Review, 1992*. Water Induced Disaster Prevention Technical Center, Lalitpur.

DPTC (1994), *Annual Disaster Review, 1993*. Water Induced Disaster Prevention Technical Center, Lalitpur.

DTPC (1996), *Annual Disaster Review, 1995*. Water Induced Disaster Prevention Technical Center, Lalitpur.

Laban P. (1978), *Field Measurements of Erosion and Sedimentation in Nepal*. Kathmandu: Ministry of Forests.

Biographical Details of Contributors

R.B. Senaka Arachchi is a Research Associate with the International Irrigation Management Institute (IIMI), Colombo, Sri Lanka. Prior to joining IIMI he worked as a Senior Research Officer with the Agrarian Research & Training Institute of Sri Lanka. Senaka Arachchi received his first degree in Economics from the University of Peradeniya, Sri Lanka and an MSc degree in Social Statistics from the University of Southampton, England. He obtained his PhD degree in Population and Human Resources from the University of Adelaide, Australia. He has been working in the field of agrarian development as a researcher for nearly 20 years.

Ela R. Bhatt is founder of the Self Employed Women's Association (SEWA) which is based in Ahmedabad; she was General Secretary of SEWA from 1972–96. She is Chair of Women's World Banking, has been a Member of Parliament and Member of the Indian Planning Commission, and received the Maysaysay Award for Community Leadership in 1977.

Mihir R. Bhatt, architect and planner, is the Director of the Disaster Mitigation Institute (DMI), which works for disaster victims and vulnerable communities in India and South Asia to build security in food, water, shelter, and work. He is a founder member of Duryog Nivaran and co-ordinates its work on vulnerability and capacity building.

Ngamindra Dahal is a Research Associate at the Nepal Water Conservation Foundation and Lecturer (part-time) at the Central Department of Hydrology and Meteorology at Tribhuvan University, Kathmandu. He founded and for several years directed a community-based organization working with street children and on child labour issues in Kathmandu. His research interests are in hydrology and meteorology, with a particular interest in the impact of climate dynamics on the sediment process in the Himalayas and its relation to society.

John Twigg is a Research fellow of the Benfield Greig Hazard Research Centre, University College, London. He specializes in Third World development and disaster mitigation, with particular interests in institutional aspects and the dissemination of information. He is a founder member of Duryog Nivaran and represents the network's interests in the UK and Europe.

Other Duryog Nivaran publications on disasters and vulnerability

For information on how to obtain these publications, write to Duryog Nivaran's Co-ordinator (the address is given at the front of this book).

Books

Bastian S., Bastian N. (ed.), *Assessing Participation: a debate from South Asia* New Delhi: Konark Publishers/Duryog Nivaran. 1996. 288pp. ISBN 81 220 0459 8. 'Participation' and 'participatory development' are fashionable words in the fields of development and disaster mitigation. This book of papers presented at a Duryog Nivaran workshop in Sri Lanka in November 1995 takes a fresh look at the topic, in theory and practice, and offers a more realistic appraisal of participatory methods.

Fernando P., Fernando V. (ed.), *South Asian Women: facing disasters, securing life*. Colombo: Duryog Nivaran. 1997. 75pp. ISBN 955 639 000 6. A collection of papers looking at the reasons why disasters affect women differently from men and studying women's responses to crisis and vulnerability. The book draws on presentations at a Duryog Nivaran seminar in Pakistan in March 1996 as well as other material.

South Asian series on vulnerability reduction

Case-studies documenting local experiences of vulnerability in South Asia are rare. This series of short booklets presents such case-studies, illustrating the pressures that make people vulnerable and setting out ways in which they are protecting themselves against disasters or in which they could be helped to do so. The following booklets have appeared or are in press:

Ariyabandu R. De S., Dharmalingam S., *Harvesting Rainwater: a means of water security in rural Sri Lanka* (June 1997)

Tyabji L., *Craft in the Aftermath of Disaster: generating independence as well as incomes* (June 1997)

Wickramarachchi P., *Food Security Strategies under Drought Hazard: a case study of Milamperumawa* (June 1997)

Nanavaty R, *Towards Building Water Security for Desert Women* (forthcoming)

A further two booklets in the series have been published in Hindi:

Rajestan mein Badh – 1 (Floods and Deserts) (March 1998)

Rajestan mein Badh – 2 (Floods and Deserts) (March 1998)